THE KINDNESS PLAN

30 Days To A Happier, Calmer and More Meaningful Life

Bill Mogolov

To my wife, Carol—this one's for you. Your love and unfailing support inspire me every single day to be a little better, a little kinder.

To my children, Andrew and Sarah, who show kindness in the way they live every day—you remind me constantly that kindness is not just something we do, but something we are.

To my grandchildren, Brady and Brooklyn—may you carry the values of kindness with you as you grow, guiding you to lead lives filled with meaning, joy, and richness.

And to the women at the Iowa Correctional Institute for Women who taught me more about kindness than I ever thought possible.

CHAPTER INSTRUCTIONS
How To Get The Most Out Of This Book

Welcome to The Kindness Plan: 30 Days to a Happier, Calmer, and More Meaningful Life. This book is designed to guide you through a 30-day journey of kindness, one step at a time. To truly benefit from this experience, here's how to approach it:

One Chapter a Day

When you reach Chapter 1, remember to read only one chapter each day. Each chapter is carefully crafted to take about six minutes to read, but it's not just about finishing quickly. The key is to let the message resonate. Resist the temptation to read ahead—giving yourself time to reflect is essential. Reading more than one chapter a day can overload you and prevent you from fully absorbing the transformative power of this journey.

Reflect and Absorb

After reading, pause and reflect on the chapter's insights.

How can you apply them in your daily life? This book is not just for reading but for living. Take the time to absorb the message and turn it into action. Each day offers a new opportunity to grow and practice kindness in small, meaningful ways.

No Pressure

If you miss a day, don't worry! Simply pick up where you left off. This is a journey at your own pace, with no pressure or deadlines. The focus is on progress, not perfection. Whenever you're ready, return to the next chapter and continue your exploration of kindness.

Commit to the Process

The more you invest in this process, the more profound the impact will be. After 30 days, you'll have gained tools and insights that can continue to enrich your life long after the book is finished.

So, take it slow, enjoy the experience, and remember: one chapter at a time.

INTRODUCTION

Learning Kindness In The Most Unlikely Place

I used to be a jerk. That's right. The author of "The Kindness Plan: 30 Days To A Happier, Calmer And More Meaningful Life" was once the last person you'd call kind. There was a time when I wasn't exactly someone people enjoyed being around. I had a knack for making situations uncomfortable....snapping at a restaurant server over a minor mistake, cutting people off mid-conversation because I thought what I had to say was more important, or turning many interactions into opportunities to talk about myself and bragging about the success I was having in my small business. I was the guy tapping his foot in the grocery store line, sighing loudly, making sure everyone knew just how much I hated waiting. What a piece of work I was!

One day, a customer came into my office and complained about the high price of one of my services. I didn't handle it well. My face turned red, and my temper flared. I lost control and angrily told her to leave and never come back. What I didn't realize at the time was that she happened to be a good friend of my mom.

Not long after, my phone rang—it was my mom. She didn't hold back. In a calm but firm tone, she made it clear just how embarrassed she felt about the way I had treated her friend. Hearing the disappointment in her voice felt like a punch to the gut. That was the moment I realized my behavior wasn't just damaging my reputation; it was also hurting the people I cared about.

Looking back, it's clear how my behavior pushed people away. I was caught up in my own world, wrapped up in my impatience, my need to be heard, and my obsession with material success. I believed I was simply being assertive or efficient, but in truth, I was acting selfishly and without consideration for others. My circle of friends kept shrinking because people naturally avoid those who make them feel insignificant, unheard, or diminished. And that was me—constantly putting my needs and my ego first, with little regard for anyone else.

Then one day, I received a call from a friend who was volunteering at a women's prison, teaching drama classes to the inmates. She spoke passionately about how rewarding the experience was, sharing stories of how the women opened up and grew through the classes. Then she asked if I'd consider volunteering to teach business classes, given that I owned a small business at the time.

My immediate response was a firm and unwavering "NO." The idea of volunteering in a prison seemed pointless to me. I was skeptical that the inmates would have any genuine interest in learning, and I was certain that we wouldn't find any common ground. The thought of stepping into that environment felt uncomfortable and foreign. I was convinced that my efforts would be wasted and that my time would be better spent elsewhere on more meaningful or productive activities. I didn't see the value in even giving it a try, as my mind was already made up. But my friend didn't give up easily.

She kept encouraging me, talking about how much of a difference I could make, not just for the inmates but for me, too. I resisted, listing every reason I could think of to avoid stepping into that unfamiliar world. But her persistence wore me down, and finally, more to stop the pestering than out of any real desire, I begrudgingly said, "Fine, I'll give it a try...but no guarantees."

Walking into the prison for the first time on a cold January night, I felt like an imposter, bracing myself for disinterest, resistance, or worse. As I moved past the heavy doors and security checks, I mentally prepared myself to stay detached and simply get through the experience. As I stood on the creaky floor of the cold and poorly insulated classroom, I found myself thinking, "What have I gotten myself into?" I wanted to leave and go home, but it was too late for that. The classroom door swung open, and one by one, the women entered. I remember thinking, "They look just like ordinary women!" Little did I know then that I would never see them as just ordinary again.

As the class began, the women surprised me. They weren't disinterested or hostile; they were engaged, curious, and eager to learn. They shared their stories, asked insightful questions, and even challenged some of my business ideas in ways I hadn't expected. Beyond that, they were kind and considerate, offering words of encouragement to each other and showing a level of empathy that was truly inspiring. They were more than just inmates—they were people with dreams, aspirations, and a genuine desire to better themselves.

I left that first class feeling something I hadn't felt in a long time: fulfillment. Genuine, deep, soul-stirring fulfillment. Not from recognition or material success, but from making a real connection and contributing to someone else's growth. The feeling lingered, and I found myself thinking about those women, their questions, and their determination long after I left. Teaching those classes soon became the highlight of my week. I ended up spending eight years teaching there—some of the very best years of my life.

Through those classes, I began to understand the true power of kindness—not just as a way to help others but as a way to heal myself. I realized that kindness isn't just an act; it's a shift in perspective, a way of seeing the world that values connection over self-interest. Teaching those classes was my first real step in unlearning my old habits and starting a journey toward a happier, calmer and more meaningful life.

And so, my journey since then hasn't been about being perfect; it's been about making a conscious choice, day by day, to put kindness into action. That's what led me to write this book—not from a pedestal of having it all figured out, but from the humility of knowing I'm still a work in progress. And it's a journey I hope you'll join me on, one act of kindness at a time.

CHAPTER 1
Random Acts of Kindness: The Power of Unexpected Joy

Imagine a world where kindness is as routine as morning coffee, where every day is sprinkled with thoughtful gestures from strangers. These spontaneous acts of generosity, known as random acts of kindness possess the extraordinary power to transform lives in ways that resonate deeply within our hearts. In this chapter, we'll dive into the magic of these unplanned moments and explore how they can create ripples of goodwill, enriching both the giver and the receiver.

The Enchantment of Unexpected Kindness

Random acts of kindness are like small bursts of magic. They occur when we step out of our own world, even briefly, to do something nice for someone else. These acts are typically unplanned, often go unnoticed, and come with no expectation of reward.

Yet, their impact can be truly profound. A simple kind gesture can brighten someone's day and offer a glimmer of hope when everything seems bleak.

Consider the story of Mark, a busy father juggling work and family responsibilities. One rainy day, while struggling with his groceries and two restless kids, he found himself stuck at a crosswalk. A stranger, noticing his predicament, offered to help carry his bags across the street. Mark was deeply moved not just by the help but by the kindness and empathy the stranger showed. For Mark, this small act was a reminder of the goodness in people and it left him feeling uplifted.

These acts don't just benefit the recipient. The giver also experiences a boost. This shared goodwill fosters a sense of connection that transcends superficial differences. When we show kindness, we encourage others to follow our example., creating a ripple effect that can spread far and wide.

How Kindness Can Transform Communities

The effects of random acts of kindness extend beyond individual interactions. They can alter the atmosphere of entire communities. When kindness becomes a norm, it creates a sense of connection and warmth. Neighborhoods become friendlier, workplaces more supportive, and people more considerate of each other. And it's not just a nice idea—research backs it up. Studies have shown that witnessing or experiencing acts of kindness releases oxytocin, a hormone that reduces stress, lowers blood pressure, and enhances overall happiness.

Imagine if everyone committed to performing one random act of kindness each day. Our world would be a tapestry of joy and human connection. Small gestures of kindness could help ease loneliness and bridge divides in a world that often feels fragmented. It serves as a strong reminder of the humanity we all share and the profound impact we can have when we choose to uplift one another.

Simple Ways to Spread Kindness

Incorporating random acts of kindness to your daily routine can be simple and fast. Here are some simple and effective ideas to get you started:

1. **Pay It Forward:** Next time you're at a coffee shop or drive-thru, consider paying for the person behind you. It's a small gesture that can make to someone's day and encourage them to spread the kindness further.

2. **Leave a Kind Note:** Write uplifting notes like "You're amazing!" or "You matter" and leave them in unexpected places—inside a library book, on a bathroom mirror, or on a coworker's desk.

3. **Give a Genuine Compliment:** Compliment a stranger on something you notice, whether it's

their outfit, their smile, or their patience. It's a simple act that can have a big impact on someone's day.

4. **Lend a Helping Hand:** Offer assistance to someone struggling with heavy bags, give up your seat on a crowded bus, or hold the door open for the person behind you.

5. **Donate to a Good Cause:** Drop off a few cans at a local food pantry or contribute to a charity you care about. Your generosity can have a lasting impact.

6. **Send a Thoughtful Message:** Reach out to someone you haven't spoken to in a while with a simple text or email to let them know you're thinking of them.

These are just a few examples, but the possibilities for kindness are endless. The key is to remain open and aware of the moments around you. Random acts of kindness don't always need to be planned—they often arise naturally when we're tuned into the world.

Finding the Right Moments

In our busy lives, it's easy to get caught up in our own concerns. But when we slow down and pay attention, we can spot countless opportunities for kindness. It's about being present and mindful of the small ways we can make a difference.

Maybe it's a grocery store cashier who seems a bit

overwhelmed and could use a kind word, or a fellow commuter who might appreciate a friendly smile. Each day is filled with chances to spread a little light if we're willing to see them. Be spontaneous and genuine. Whether it's a grand gesture or a small, quiet act, the heart behind it is what truly matters.

Wrapping It Up

Random acts of kindness remind us that even the tiniest actions can make a significant difference.They help us connect with others, build empathy, and bring a bit of brightness into someone else's day. By embracing these moments of goodness, we contribute to a kinder, more compassionate world—one surprise moment of joy at a time.

Call to Action

Today, I challenge you to perform one random act of kindness in the next 24 hours. It doesn't have to be elaborate—just something that brings a bit of joy to someone else's day. Hold the door open, share a sincere compliment, pay for a coffee, or send a thoughtful message.

Keep your eyes open for those little opportunities that might otherwise pass you by. Kindness is a powerful force that starts with these small, deliberate actions. By stepping outside your routine and focusing on someone else's happiness, you have the power to create a ripple effect of goodness.

So go ahead—spread a little unexpected joy today. You

might be surprised by how it brightens someone else's day and fills your own with a sense of purpose and connection. Let's start a chain reaction of kindness, one small act at a time.

CHAPTER 2
Listening With Your Heart:
The Gift of Being Present

Listening is one of the most profound acts of kindness, and yet, it often goes unnoticed. In our fast-paced, always-connected world, with notifications pinging constantly and a never-ending list of tasks demanding our attention, the simple act of truly listening has become rare. When you listen with your heart, you're not just hearing words; you're offering your full attention, with an open mind and a compassionate spirit. It's about being genuinely present for another person, without rushing to provide solutions or advice.

Why Listening Matters More Than You Think

Listening with intention takes effort. It requires setting aside your own thoughts, opinions, and reactions to create space for someone else's experiences and emotions. It means giving them the freedom to share their story without fear of judgment or interruption. This chapter explores why listening is such a vital aspect of kindness and how it can significantly affect both your life and the lives of those around you.

The Difference Between Offering Advice and Truly Listening

When someone comes to us with a problem, our first instinct is often to jump in with advice. We want to help; we feel compelled to fix things or make it all better. However, this approach can unintentionally send the message that we aren't fully hearing what the person is trying to communicate. Offering advice can sometimes feel like taking control of the conversation, steering it towards our own experiences or opinions. It may make the other person feel as though they must take the advice or feel inadequate if they choose not to.

On the other hand, a true listener provides a non-judgmental, supportive space where someone can express their thoughts and feelings freely. This kind of listener isn't there to solve the problem but to offer empathy and understanding. They don't interrupt, don't shift the focus back to themselves, and instead ask open-ended questions that help the speaker explore their own feelings and thoughts more deeply.

Listening with empathy is about recognizing and acknowledging what the other person is feeling. It could be as simple as saying, "That sounds really difficult," or "I'm here for you." This kind of affirmation lets the speaker know that their emotions are valid and that they're not alone. By doing this, we help create a healing space where the person feels genuinely understood.

Real-Life Examples: When Listening Makes All the Difference

Consider these everyday scenarios where listening can make a profound difference:

1. **A Friend Going Through a Breakup:** When a friend is dealing with the end of a relationship, they often just need someone to hear them out. They might not be looking for advice on how to move on or what to do next. Instead, by simply being there, listening without judgment, and allowing them to share their pain, you're providing them the first step toward healing.

2. **A Colleague Feeling Overwhelmed at Work:** In a high-pressure work environment, a listening ear can be incredibly valuable. When a coworker is feeling overwhelmed, stressed, or burnt out, just acknowledging their experience can make them feel less alone and more supported. It can help reduce their stress and create a sense of camaraderie and trust among colleagues.

3. **A Family Member Facing a Difficult Decision:** Whether it's a choice about health, finances, or a personal matter, listening without judgment can help a loved one feel more confident in their

decision-making. It shows that you trust their ability to handle their own situation and that you'll be there to support them no matter what they decide. Sometimes, just being there to listen to their fears and uncertainties can make them feel stronger and more capable.

4. **A Child Expressing Anxiety:** When a child shares their worries, it's easy to dismiss them as small or insignificant. However, listening without dismissing their fears validates their feelings and teaches them that it's okay to talk about what's on their mind. This kind of listening helps build their confidence and establishes a foundation of trust and understanding that will last a lifetime.

The Ripple Effect of Heartfelt Listening

Listening builds trust and strengthens relationships. When you genuinely listen to someone, you demonstrate that you value them and their experiences. Relationships thrive when both people feel seen, heard, and respected. Listening also helps to reduce misunderstandings and conflicts, creating a safe space where people feel comfortable being themselves and sharing openly.

Think about a time when someone really listened to you. How did it make you feel? Did you feel respected, valued, or understood? Now imagine the impact you can have on others when you offer the same gift of listening with your heart.

Practical Steps to Become a Better Listener

Becoming a better listener takes practice, but the rewards are immense. Here are a few practical steps to help you get started:

1. **Put Away Distractions:** Whether it's your phone, your laptop, or your own thoughts, set them aside when someone is speaking to you. Maintain eye contact and show that you are fully present and actively engaged in the conversation.

2. **Avoid The Temptation To Interrupt Or Suggest Solutions.:** Instead of jumping in with advice or your own stories, allow the other person to share at their own pace. If you feel the urge to speak, remind yourself that your role is to listen, not to fix.

3. **Ask Open-Ended Questions:** Encourage deeper conversation by asking questions that prompt reflection, such as "How did that make you feel?" or "What do you think you'll do next?" This shows that you're interested in their perspective and helps them explore their own thoughts and feelings more fully.

4. **Echo What You Hear:** Restating or summarizing the other person's words can demonstrate that you are genuinely listening. For example, "It sounds like you're feeling really frustrated about that situation. Is that right?"

5. **Offer Empathy, Not Sympathy:** Instead of saying, "I'm sorry you're going through this," try, "That sounds really tough. I'm here for you." Empathy shows that you're trying to understand their feelings, not just offering pity.

Call to Action: Practice Heartfelt Listening

This week, I challenge you to be a listener, not an advice giver. Pick at least one conversations where you choose to listen with your whole heart. Put away any distractions, make eye contact, and actively listen by reflecting back what the person has said to ensure you understand. Resist the urge to jump in with your own stories or advice.

Afterward, take a moment to reflect on how this experience felt for both you and the other person. Did they open up more? Did you feel a deeper connection or understanding? Write down any changes you noticed in your relationships or how people responded to you.

By practicing heartfelt listening, you'll discover firsthand the transformative power of this simple yet profound act of kindness. You might find that you not only understand others better but also feel more connected and grounded in your relationships. Listening with your heart is a gift you give to others—and to yourself.

CHAPTER 3
Compliments that Count: Uplifting Others with Words

There's something truly magical about a genuine compliment. It can lift someone's spirits, make them feel valued, and even help forge connections that last a lifetime. While compliments may seem small, when they are sincere and thoughtful, they can have a profound impact. In our fast-paced world, where everyone is juggling endless responsibilities, taking a moment to offer a kind word can be like dropping a pebble into a pond—creating ripples that spread far and wide.

The Secret to a Good Compliment

Not all compliments are created equal. The most meaningful ones go beyond the typical "Nice outfit!" or "Good job!" While these are pleasant to hear, they often don't leave a lasting impression. To truly uplift someone, a compliment needs to be real, specific, and heartfelt.

Think back to a time when someone complimented you in a way that stayed with you. Maybe a teacher praised your unique way of thinking, a friend admired your perseverance, or a colleague noticed your knack for problem-solving. These compliments resonate because they reflect something true and personal about who we are—something we may not even recognize in ourselves. They make us feel genuinely appreciated in a way that generic praise never could.

Why Compliments Matter

Compliments are like little gifts we can give each other —they don't cost anything, but they're incredibly valuable. They affirm that we're doing something right, that who we are matters. Studies have even shown that receiving a compliment lights up the same part of the brain as receiving a monetary reward. That's how powerful our words can be!

When we sincerely compliment someone, we do more than just brighten their day; we help boost their confidence and self-esteem. We're saying, "I see you. I appreciate you. You matter." This is especially impactful for people who might feel overlooked or undervalued. A single compliment can shift someone's perspective, lift their spirits, and help them see themselves in a more positive light.

How to Give Compliments That Really Count

If you want your compliments to truly make a

difference, focus on three key elements: be specific, be sincere, and be thoughtful.

1. Be Specific: Instead of saying, "You're amazing," try, "I really admire how you handled that challenging situation today with such grace." The more specific you are, the more genuine your compliment will feel. It shows you're paying attention, which makes the person feel truly seen.

2. Be Sincere: Speak from the heart. Don't feel like you have to force a compliment just for the sake of it. If you're struggling to find the right words, take a moment to think about the qualities or actions you genuinely admire in the person. Your words should reflect what you honestly feel.

3. Be Thoughtful: Tailor your compliment to the person. What matters to one person may not mean as much to another. Consider what would be most meaningful to them. Is it their kindness, their creativity, or their tenacity? When your compliment aligns with their values or personality, it becomes far more impactful.

Examples of Compliments That Make a Difference

Here are some examples of compliments that go beyond the surface and truly uplift:

1. **To a Friend Who Listens Well:**" You have this incredible ability to make people feel truly understood. Your listening skills are a rare and beautiful gift."

2. **To a Colleague Who Goes the Extra Mile:**" I noticed all the effort you put into preparing for that meeting. Your attention to detail really made a difference and didn't go unnoticed."

3. **To a Family Member Showing Resilience:**" I've seen how you've been dealing with everything lately, and I'm genuinely inspired by your strength and determination to keep going."

4. **To a Stranger Who Brightened Your Day:**" Your friendly smile just made my day better. I didn't realize how much I needed that. Thank you!"

5. **To a Child Showing Kindness:**" I saw how you helped your classmate today. That was such a thoughtful thing to do, and it shows what a kind person you are becoming."

The Magic of Unexpected Compliments

While complimenting those we know is valuable, there's something uniquely special about complimenting a stranger. It catches them by surprise and can have an even more significant impact. Think about the cashier at the grocery store who's been standing all day or the person in line next to you who looks a bit down. A simple, sincere compliment can be a bright spot in their day, reminding them that kindness still exists in the world, even from unexpected places.

The next time you're out, look for opportunities to compliment someone genuinely. You might be amazed at how it lifts their mood—and yours, too. Often, giving a compliment feels just as good as receiving one.

How Kind Words Spread

When we offer a meaningful compliment, we're not just making someone else feel good; we're also spreading kindness in our community. Compliments can create a ripple effect—when someone feels valued and appreciated, they're more likely to pass that kindness on to others. This is how kindness spreads, one small gesture at a time.

Picture a workplace where compliments are given freely and sincerely. People feel valued, morale improves, and teamwork becomes stronger. Or imagine a family where compliments are a natural part of daily conversation. Relationships grow deeper, and the home becomes a space filled with encouragement and support. By choosing to uplift others with our words, we help make the world a little warmer, a little more connected, and a lot more loving.

Don't Forget to Compliment Yourself

Remember, kindness isn't just something we extend to others—it's something we need to offer ourselves, too. How often do you take a moment to give yourself a compliment? Most of us are quick to criticize our flaws and slow to recognize our strengths.

Take a moment to give yourself a compliment today.

Think about what you're proud of, what makes you unique, or how you've handled a difficult situation recently. By being kind to ourselves, we create a solid foundation to genuinely uplift others.

Call to Action: Spread Those Compliments!

This week, challenge yourself to give three meaningful compliments each day. Look for opportunities in your daily interactions—whether at work, at home, or with strangers. Remember to be specific, sincere, and thoughtful. Notice how these compliments are received and how they make you feel, too.

Compliments are a simple but powerful way to practice kindness. By taking the time to uplift others with our words, we create a world where everyone feels a little more appreciated, a little more seen, and a lot more loved.

So, let's start a kindness revolution—one compliment at a time.

CHAPTER 4

The Gift of Patience: Staying Grounded in Tough Times

We've all heard the saying, "Patience is a virtue," but let's be honest—staying patient is much easier said than done. We live in a world where everything happens in an instant. We're used to quick replies, same-day deliveries, and fast solutions for almost every problem. So, when life throws a situation at us that requires waiting or challenges our tolerance, it's tempting to lose our cool. But here's the truth: patience is a superpower, and it's one of the kindest things we can practice, both for ourselves and for others.

Why Patience is a Form of Kindness

Patience is not just about waiting without complaining or staying calm when things go wrong —it's about extending grace to ourselves and those around us. It means giving others the time and space to be human, to make mistakes, and to grow at their own pace. When we're patient, we're saying, "I'm here for you. I'm not in a rush to change you or the situation. I'm okay with letting things unfold as they're meant to."

Think about how it feels when someone is patient with you. Maybe you made a mistake at work, and instead of getting an angry reaction, your boss calmly helps you figure out what went wrong. Or perhaps you're running late to meet a friend, and instead of a frown, they greet you with a smile. Those moments feel like a breath of fresh air. That's the power of patience—it creates a sense of safety and understanding that makes even the most stressful situations feel a little lighter.

The Power of Taking a Pause

When things go sideways—like when you're stuck in traffic, dealing with a difficult conversation, or overwhelmed by a never-ending to-do list—our first instinct is often to react quickly. But what if, instead, we chose to pause? Just a brief moment to take a deep breath, collect our thoughts, and remind ourselves that we don't have to respond immediately.

That pause can be transformative. It gives us a chance to calm down, think clearly, and respond with kindness instead of frustration. It's not about ignoring our feelings or pretending everything is okay when it's not. It's about giving ourselves a little grace and choosing to respond in a way that feels good to both us and those around us.

Real-Life Example: Imagine you're at the airport, and your flight gets delayed. Your first reaction might be to feel annoyed or angry. But instead, you take a moment to breathe, acknowledge your frustration, and then think about how you can use this unexpected time. Maybe you catch up on a book you've been meaning to read, call a friend, or simply take some time to relax. That pause allows you to make a conscious choice about how you respond to the situation.

Practicing Patience with Ourselves

Let's face it—sometimes, the hardest person to be patient with is ourselves. We set high expectations and criticize ourselves when we don't meet them. We rush through our days, constantly looking for the next thing to check off our list, and when things don't go as planned, we get frustrated or disappointed.

But what if we treated ourselves with the same patience we'd offer a good friend? What if we were kinder to ourselves when we make a mistake or fall behind? Practicing patience with ourselves means recognizing that we're human, that growth takes time, and that it's okay to move forward one step at a time.

Practical Tip: The next time you find yourself being hard on yourself, try saying, "It's okay. I'm doing the best I can." Give yourself permission to be imperfect and to take things one day at a time. This small shift in mindset can reduce stress and help you approach your goals with a more positive attitude.

Finding Patience in Everyday Moments

Patience doesn't have to be reserved for big challenges; it can be practiced in the small moments of everyday life. It's waiting in line at the grocery store without grumbling. It's letting your partner finish their story without interrupting. It's giving your kids the time they need to tie their shoes or figure out a homework problem on their own. These small acts of patience add up and create an environment of calm and kindness.

Patience with Others: Giving People Room to Grow

We all have people in our lives who test our patience —a colleague who misses deadlines, a friend who's always late, or a family member who knows how to push our buttons. It's easy to get frustrated and want to snap, but what if we saw these moments as opportunities to practice patience?

Giving others the space to be themselves, flaws and all, is a powerful act of kindness. It's about recognizing that everyone is on their journey, dealing with their own challenges, and doing the best they can with what they have. When we offer patience, we're letting them know that it's okay to be human, to take their time, and to learn and grow at their own pace.

Practical Advice: Next time you find yourself feeling impatient with someone, try to see things from their perspective. Consider what they might be going through and remind yourself that they, like you, are just trying to navigate life's challenges. A slight change in perspective can greatly influence your response.

The Benefits of Patience

Here's the great thing about practicing patience: it's not just good for others; it's good for us too. When we're patient, we're less stressed, more present, and more in tune with what's happening around us. We become better listeners, more compassionate friends, and kinder humans. Plus, being patient helps us build stronger relationships because people feel safe and comfortable around us—they know we're not going to snap or rush them.

Call to Action: Cultivating Patience

This week, try practicing patience in different areas of your life. Start small—maybe it's taking a few deep breaths before responding when someone annoys you, or giving yourself grace when things don't go as planned. Notice how it feels to be patient with yourself and others. Does it make your day a little less stressful? Do you feel more connected to those around you?

Patience is like a muscle—the more you use it, the stronger it gets. And the best part? Every time you choose patience, you're choosing kindness, both for yourself and for others.

CHAPTER 5

From the Heart: The Transformative Power of a Smile

Have you ever observed how a smile can immediately lighten the mood? It's a small gesture, yet its impact can be profound. A smile has the power to transform our interactions, boost our own mood, and spread kindness in ways we might not even realize. In this chapter, we'll explore the transformative power of a smile and how this simple act of kindness can create ripples of positivity in our lives and the lives of others.

The Science of Smiling

Before diving into practical advice, let's start with some fascinating science. When you smile, your brain releases chemicals like endorphins and serotonin, which serve as natural mood lifters. These mood enhancing chemicals help in reducing stress and anxiety, making you feel happier and more relaxed. Interestingly, the mere act of smiling, even if you're not feeling particularly joyful, can trick your brain into feeling better. It's as if your face is sending a message to your brain: "Everything's okay!"

Moreover, smiling is contagious. A smile is contagious; when you share one with someone, they're likely to return it., creating a cycle of positivity. This ripple effect means that one smile can spread to many people, brightening their day and enhancing social connections. Studies have shown that seeing a smiling face activates the brain's reward centers, making us feel happier and more connected. It's a simple but powerful tool for building personal connections and nurturing a sense of community.

Practical Ways to Harness the Power of Your Smile

Now that we've seen how powerful a smile can be, how can you make the most of this simple act of kindness? Here are some practical tips:

1. **Smile Genuinely**: A genuine smile is more impactful than a forced one. To make your smile authentic, think of something that brings you joy— perhaps a fond memory or a happy thought. This will naturally reflect in your smile and make it more sincere. Authenticity is key; a real smile lights up your entire face and communicates warmth and sincerity.

2. **Use Your Smile in Difficult Situations**: When you're dealing with challenging situations or difficult people, try to maintain a calm and genuine

smile. It can help defuse tension and foster a more positive atmosphere. Smiling doesn't mean ignoring the problem, but it can make conversations more constructive and less confrontational. It acts as a social lubricant that makes it easier to navigate conflicts and misunderstandings.

3. **Smile at Strangers**: It's easy to smile at friends and family, but don't forget to extend this kindness to strangers. Whether it's a cashier, a passerby, or a fellow commuter, a smile can brighten someone's day and make them feel acknowledged. A smile from a stranger can be surprisingly uplifting and may even make someone's day better, creating a ripple effect of positivity.

4. **Practice Smiling in the Mirror**: If you're not used to smiling often, practice in front of the mirror. This will help you become more comfortable with the expression and make it easier to share with others. Observing your smile and adjusting it to feel more natural can help you become more accustomed to smiling frequently.

5. **Pair Your Smile with Kind Words**: Enhance the power of your smile by pairing it with kind words or compliments. For example, telling someone, "I appreciate your help today," while smiling, can make the compliment even more impactful. The combination of a smile and positive words can create a powerful emotional boost for both you and the recipient.

6. Make Smiling a Habit: Incorporate smiling into your daily routine. Whether it's starting your day with a smile or making it a point to smile at your loved ones, turning this into a habit will help you naturally spread more positivity. The more you smile, the more natural it will become, and the more benefits you'll experience both emotionally and socially.

The Contagious Effect of Smiling

One of the most beautiful aspects of a smile is its contagious effect. When you smile at someone, it not only affects their mood but can also influence how they interact with others. Imagine a world where everyone made an effort to smile more. The collective impact would be enormous—creating a more friendly, welcoming, and positive environment.

Think about how you can be a catalyst for this ripple effect. Each smile you share has the potential to spread joy, lift spirits, and foster connections. By making smiling a part of your daily life, you're contributing to a wave of kindness that can touch countless lives. The act of smiling can transform an ordinary interaction into a memorable and uplifting experience for both you and the other person.

Call to Action: Smile and See the Change

This week, I challenge you to harness the transformative power of your smile. Start by paying attention to how often you smile and consciously make an effort to share your smile more freely. Begin with those closest to you—family members, friends, and colleagues. Then, expand to strangers you encounter throughout your day.

Notice the impact your smile has on others. Observe how it affects their reactions and your own mood. Reflect on how this simple gesture can create a ripple of positivity, making both your world and theirs a little brighter.

By embracing the power of your smile, you're not just spreading kindness—you're also enhancing your own well-being and contributing to a more positive atmosphere wherever you go. Let your smile be a beacon of joy and connection. Share it generously, and watch how it transforms your life and the lives of those around you.

Smiling is one of the simplest, yet most powerful acts of kindness. It requires no special skills, no elaborate plans—just the willingness to share a moment of warmth and connection. So, let's make a habit of smiling and creating a world where every day is a little brighter and more welcoming, one smile at a time.

CHAPTER 6
Loving Yourself: A Kindness Often Overlooked

When we think about kindness, we usually picture the warmth we extend to others—a comforting hug, a thoughtful gesture, or a kind word. But there is one person who often gets left out of our circle of kindness: ourselves. In a world that constantly pushes us to do more, be more, and give more, it's easy to forget that we are also deserving of the compassion we so freely offer to others.

Loving yourself is an act of kindness that is often overlooked. It's not about being selfish or self-centered; it's about recognizing your own worth and treating yourself with the same care and understanding that you extend to those around you. In this chapter, we'll explore the importance of self-kindness, share practical ways to practice it, and look at how this powerful act can transform your life from the inside out.

Why Self-Kindness Matters

Picture your best friend facing a rough patch—overwhelmed at work, struggling with a setback, or feeling down. How would you react? Likely, you'd offer supportive words, suggest they take a break, or remind them of their achievements. Now, consider how you treat yourself in similar circumstances. Do you extend the same compassion to yourself, or are you your own harshest critic? Reflect on this: are you as kind and understanding toward yourself as you would be to a friend in need?

For many of us, the answer is clear: we are far more forgiving and understanding toward others than we are toward ourselves. We hold ourselves to impossible standards, criticize our every mistake, and push ourselves to exhaustion. But here's the truth: if you wouldn't speak to a friend that way, why speak to yourself like that?

Self-kindness matters because it lays the foundation for how we experience the world. When we are kind to ourselves, we are more resilient in facing stress and bouncing back from setbacks, and maintaining healthy relationships. It helps us build resilience and a sense of inner peace that no external validation can provide.

Real-Life Example: Kathryn's Journey to Self-Compassion

Consider Kathryn, a sales executive who had always

prided herself on her drive and work ethic.. For years, she struggled to maintain long hours, a busy family life, and a packed social calendar. But one day, Kathryn hit a wall. She found herself feeling constantly exhausted, irritable, and unmotivated. She began to criticize herself for not being productive enough, not being a better mother, or not being able to do it all.

After months of this self-critical spiral, Kathryn decided to make a change. She realized that she had been kinder to everyone around her than she had ever been to herself. She began a simple daily regimen: every morning, she would spend five minutes writing down three things she appreciated about herself. Some days, it was as basic as "I got out of bed" or "I made a healthy breakfast." Other days, it was "I handled that sales presentation well" or "I was patient with my children."

At first, it felt strange and even uncomfortable. But over time, Kathryn noticed a shift. She started to feel more at ease, less stressed, and more capable of handling challenges. She still had bad days, but she was quicker to forgive herself and move on. By practicing self-kindness, she discovered a newfound sense of balance and inner strength.

Practical Ways to Practice Self-Kindness

So, how can you start to show yourself the kindness you deserve? Here are some practical steps to help you begin:

1. **Speak to Yourself Like a Friend**: Pay attention to your inner dialogue. If you find yourself being overly critical, pause and ask yourself, "Would I say this to a friend?" If the answer is no, rephrase it with a more compassionate tone. For example, instead of saying, "I'm such a failure for making that mistake," try, "I made a mistake, but I'm learning and growing from it."

2. **Set Realistic Expectations**: It's great to have goals and aspirations, but be mindful of setting expectations that are realistic and achievable. Recognize that it's okay not to be perfect. Give yourself permission to make mistakes and learn from them, rather than punishing yourself for every misstep.

3. **Create Time for Self-Care**: Self-care is more than just bubble baths and spa days—it's about making time for activities that nurture your mind, body, and soul. This could mean taking a walk in nature, reading a book, meditating, or simply taking a nap. Schedule these activities into your week as you would any important appointment.

4. **Celebrate Your Achievements, Big and Small**: Make it a habit to celebrate your accomplishments, no matter how small they may seem. Did you manage to drink enough water today? Great! Did you finally tackle that project you've been putting off? Fantastic! Acknowledging these wins helps build a positive mindset and reinforces your worth.

5. **Practice Self-Compassion Exercises**: Activities like journaling, meditation, or mindfulness exercises can help cultivate a kinder relationship with yourself. For example, try a loving-kindness meditation, where you silently repeat phrases like "May I be happy, may I be healthy, may I be at peace" while focusing on yourself.

6. **Forgive Yourself**: Holding onto guilt or shame for past mistakes can be a heavy burden. Practice forgiving yourself for things you regret, just as you would forgive someone else. Remind yourself that everyone makes mistakes, and it's all part of the human experience.

7. **Ask for Help When Needed**: Recognize that it's okay to seek support. Whether it's talking to a therapist, reaching out to a friend, or asking for help with a task, asking for help is a sign of strength, not weakness.

The Benefits of Loving Yourself

When you practice kindness toward yourself, it doesn't just benefit you; it impacts those around you as well. When you are at peace with yourself, you bring a sense of calm and positivity into your relationships. You become more patient, understanding, and compassionate toward others because you have given those gifts to yourself first.

Think of it like this: you can't pour from an empty cup. By filling your own cup with self-love and compassion, you have more to give to others. It's not about being self-centered; it's about being self-aware and understanding that your well-being is essential for a kind and fulfilling life.

Call to Action: Start a Self-Kindness Ritual

This week, I encourage you to start a simple self-kindness ritual. Set aside five minutes each day to do something kind for yourself. It could be writing down three things you appreciate about yourself, taking a few deep breaths when you're feeling stressed, or giving yourself a compliment in the mirror.

Notice how these small acts of self-love make you feel over time. Do you feel more at ease, more resilient, or more joyful? Remember, being kind to yourself is not a luxury—it's a necessity. By loving yourself, you lay the foundation for a life filled with kindness, both for yourself and for others.

So, let's begin. Take that first step towards self-kindness today and watch how it transforms not just your life, but the lives of everyone around you.

CHAPTER 7
Gentle Gestures: Offering Kindness To The Ill

Illness can feel like a storm, suddenly arriving without warning and changing everything in its path. For those who are sick, even the simplest tasks can become overwhelming, and days that used to feel ordinary are now filled with uncertainty and struggle. In these moments, kindness can become a lifeline—an anchor in the middle of a turbulent sea. When someone is dealing with illness, whether it's a cold that lingers too long or a serious medical condition, our kindness can provide comfort, hope, and a sense of connection.

But how do we offer kindness in a way that truly supports someone who is unwell? It's not always easy to know what to do or say. This chapter will explore gentle gestures that can make a significant difference to someone who is sick, bringing warmth and care to their journey through illness.

1. The Power of Presence: Simply Being There

One of the simplest yet most profound gifts you can give to someone who is sick is your presence. Being there doesn't always mean being physically present—though it can. It also means showing up emotionally and letting them know they are not alone. You don't need to have all the right words or solutions. Sometimes, just sitting quietly, listening, or holding their hand can speak volumes.

If you can't be there in person, reach out with a phone call or a video chat. Even a short message saying, "I'm thinking of you," can remind someone that they matter and are cared for. Often, the best support comes not from grand gestures but from small, consistent acts that say, "I'm here with you through this."

2. Practical Help: Lightening the Load

When someone is sick, even the most mundane daily tasks can feel like mountains. Offering practical help can be an incredibly kind gesture that eases their burden. This might mean delivering a meal, picking up groceries, or helping with chores around the house. Consider what you know about the person and what might be most helpful to them.

If you're unsure, ask, "What would make things a bit easier for you right now?" Offer specific options like, "Would it help if I walked your dog, picked up your prescription, or cleaned your kitchen?" This can make it easier for them to accept your offer because it shows you genuinely want to help in a way that meets their needs.

3. Thoughtful Tokens: Small Gestures with Big Impact

Sometimes, the smallest things make the biggest impact. A handwritten card, a bouquet of flowers, or a care package tailored to their preferences can all bring a smile and remind them that they are loved and valued. Think about what would make them feel seen and special. If they love a certain type of tea, include that in your package. If they have a favorite movie, consider sending it with some popcorn for a cozy night in.

For those who might not be able to enjoy traditional gifts, like food or flowers, think creatively. A playlist of soothing music, a collection of uplifting quotes, or a beautiful book of poetry can also provide comfort and joy. The thought and care you put into these small gifts can mean far more than the items themselves.

4. Listen with Empathy: The Gift of Your Ears

When people are sick, they often feel unheard or misunderstood. One of the best gifts you can offer is to listen—really listen. Let them share their fears, frustrations, or whatever they need to talk about without trying to fix or solve anything. Practice active listening by nodding, maintaining eye contact, and responding with empathy. You might say, "That

BILLMOGOLOV

sounds really tough," or "I'm here for you," to show you understand and care about what they're going through.

Avoid jumping in with advice unless asked. Sometimes, people just need a safe space to express themselves without feeling like they need to defend their emotions or experiences. Your compassionate listening can be a powerful source of comfort and healing.

5. Respect Their Boundaries: Kindness Is Respectful

It's important to remember that everyone's experience of illness is different. Some people may want company, while others may need solitude. Some might want to talk about their illness; others may prefer to focus on something else entirely. Always ask what they're comfortable with and respect their wishes.

Check in before visiting or sending anything. A simple message like, "I'd love to come by if you're up for it, but no pressure," allows them to make the decision without feeling obligated. Be understanding if they need to cancel plans or if they don't have the energy to respond right away. Your flexibility and understanding are forms of kindness in themselves.

6. Offer Encouragement: Words That Heal

Words can be incredibly powerful, especially

46

when someone is feeling low. A few words of encouragement can provide hope and strength. Keep your messages sincere and positive without being overly cheerful. A simple "You're doing so great," "I believe in you," or "Take it one day at a time" can make a big difference. Share uplifting stories or experiences, but be mindful not to minimize what they are going through.

If they are facing a long-term illness, regular messages of encouragement can help them feel supported over the long haul. Consistency shows that you are there for them, not just at the start, but throughout their journey.

7. Create Comfort: A Soothing Environment

If you are close enough to the person to visit, think about how you can create a comfortable, soothing environment for them. Bring a soft blanket, their favorite snacks, or set up a cozy space with pillows and their favorite movies or shows. Help them with simple tasks like fluffing pillows or fetching water. Think about what would make their space feel more restful and comforting.

Sometimes, offering to help with a small task like organizing medications or setting up a cozy reading corner can show them that you're thinking about their comfort and well-being in a very practical way.

Call to Action: A Kindness Challenge

Now, it's your turn to make a difference. Think of

someone in your life who might be struggling with an illness—whether it's a cold, a chronic condition, or something in between. Reach out to them today. Send a message, drop off a meal, or offer a listening ear. Choose one small act of kindness you can do and commit to doing it within the next 24 hours.

Remember, you don't have to do something elaborate. Even the tiniest act can make a significant difference when it comes from the heart. Your kindness might just be the light they need in a difficult time.

By choosing to offer gentle gestures, you are showing compassion, love, and support to someone who needs it most. And in doing so, you'll find that your kindness not only transforms their day—but it also enriches your own.

CHAPTER 8
Embracing Compassion With Your Partner

Amid the constant rush and demands of our everyday lives, it's easy to forget the small, tender gestures that keep a relationship strong and vibrant. Whether you've been with your partner for a few months or several decades, there's one essential element that can transform your bond and breathe new life into your relationship: kindness.

Kindness might seem like a soft concept—something warm and fuzzy, but maybe not all that powerful. Yet, it is the quiet force that holds a relationship together when everything else feels like it's falling apart. It is the glue that binds two people, making them feel seen, valued, and cherished. Imagine kindness as the unsung hero in your love story, patiently waiting to be noticed and embraced. The good news? You can start infusing more kindness into your relationship today, right now, with simple acts that speak volumes.

Why Kindness Matters in Relationships

You may have heard the phrase, "Love is a verb." It means that love isn't just a feeling; it's an action. It's something you do every day through your words, your touch, and your attention. At its core, kindness is an expression of love—a way of saying, "I care about you," without needing to say anything at all.

Kindness builds trust, and trust is the foundation of any strong relationship. When we show kindness to our partner, we're telling them that they are safe with us, that they matter, and that their feelings are valid. This feeling of security creates an environment where love can thrive.

Consider this: When was the last time you went out of your way to do something kind for your partner without expecting anything in return? When was the last time you complimented them sincerely or surprised them with their favorite snack? If it's been a while, don't worry—you're not alone. But by making small, consistent efforts, you can change the course of your relationship and bring back that sense of connection and joy.

The Power of Small Acts of Kindness

Big gestures—like planning a surprise vacation or buying an expensive gift—can certainly make an impact, but it's the small, everyday acts of kindness that truly keep the spark alive. These little moments, when accumulated over time, form the bedrock of a loving and lasting relationship. Here are a few practical examples:

1. **Listen with Intent**: When your partner is speaking, give them your full attention. Put down your phone, make eye contact, and show genuine interest in what they are saying. Listening is one of the most powerful forms of kindness because it makes your partner feel valued and understood.

2. **Say Thank You**: Don't underestimate the power of gratitude. A simple "thank you" for making dinner, doing the laundry, or just being there can go a long way. Gratitude reinforces positive behavior and encourages both of you to keep contributing to the relationship.

3. **Leave Love Notes**: This may sound old-fashioned, but leaving little notes for your partner to find can add a delightful surprise to their day. It might be a sticky note on the bathroom mirror. saying, "I love you," or a card in their lunch bag saying, "You make my life better." These tiny gestures of kindness remind your partner that you're thinking of them, even when you're apart.

4. **Offer Help Without Being Asked**: Notice when your partner seems overwhelmed or stressed. Step in and offer to help without waiting to be asked. Whether it's doing a chore they dislike or giving them a back rub after a long day, these actions speak louder than words.

5. Celebrate Their Wins: Whether it's a big promotion or a small personal victory, celebrate your partner's achievements. Make them feel special, even if it's something as simple as preparing their favorite meal or toasting to their success at dinner.

Creating a Culture of Kindness in Your Relationship

To build a relationship rooted in kindness, both partners need to be committed to making kindness a priority. This doesn't mean you'll never argue or have disagreements; it means that even during tough times, you approach each other with respect and compassion.

Here are some ways to create a culture of kindness in your relationship:

1. **Speak with Gentle Honesty**: Being honest doesn't have to mean being harsh. You can express your feelings openly while being mindful of your partner's emotions. Choose words that are loving and constructive, not hurtful or critical.

2. **Practice Patience**: Everyone has moments when they're not their best selves. Maybe your partner had a rough day at work, or they're dealing with personal stress. Practicing patience allows you to be kind, even when it's challenging.

3. **Forgive Quickly**: Holding onto resentment or past grievances only creates distance between you and your partner. When you choose to

forgive and let go, you open the door to healing and deeper connection.

4. **Be Thoughtful and Considerate**: Being kind in a relationship means being considerate of your partner's needs and desires. If they've had a hard day, offer comfort. If they're excited about something, celebrate with them. Thoughtfulness goes hand-in-hand with kindness.

Kindness as a Habit: Building the Practice Together

Making kindness a daily habit in your relationship might require some conscious effort at first, but it will soon become second nature. One helpful approach is to start a daily practice of reflecting on one kind thing you did for your partner and one kind thing they did for you. Share these moments with each other before bed. This simple ritual can reinforce positive behavior and keep you both aware of the kindness you bring into each other's lives.Another idea is to create a "kindness jar." Write down acts of kindness on small pieces of paper, and each day, pick one to do for your partner. It could be something as simple as making their favorite coffee in the morning or planning a surprise date night. The key is to keep the element of surprise and joy alive in your relationship.

Call to Action: Start Small, Start Today

Kindness is the heartbeat of love. It is what turns an ordinary relationship into an extraordinary one.

Begin today by choosing one small act of kindness you can do for your partner. Maybe it's a compliment, an unexpected hug, or simply listening with an open heart. Whatever it is, commit to doing it with genuine love and intention.

Over time, these small acts of kindness will create a ripple effect, deepening your bond and bringing you closer together. Remember, it's not about perfection but about making an effort to cherish each other daily. Let kindness be the key to unlocking the fullest potential of your love story.

CHAPTER 9
Kindness At Home

Kindness often starts at home. Our families are the first places where we learn about love, empathy, and how to relate to others. They are our first teachers and our first friends. Yet, despite our best intentions, we sometimes take those closest to us for granted. The stress of daily life, misunderstandings, and busy schedules can make it easy to forget the importance of showing kindness to the people we love most.

But imagine a home where kindness is the rule, not the exception—a place where family members support, uplift, and truly listen to one another. Creating a culture of kindness at home is one of the most powerful things we can do for ourselves and our loved ones. It's a gift that keeps giving, shaping us into better versions of ourselves and setting an example for future generations.

The Ripple Effect of Kindness in Families

Kindness in the family has a profound impact that

extends far beyond our front doors. When kindness becomes a daily practice, it creates a ripple effect that reaches friends, neighbors, and even strangers. A child who grows up in a kind household is more likely to treat others with kindness, carry that value into adulthood, and pass it on to their children.

Think about how a simple act of kindness, like a comforting hug or a thoughtful note, can transform a person's day. Now, imagine the impact of making those moments a regular part of family life. When kindness is woven into the fabric of our family, it nurtures a sense of security and belonging that can withstand even the toughest challenges.

Simple Acts of Kindness at Home

Building a foundation of kindness at home doesn't require grand gestures or elaborate plans. In fact, it's the small, everyday acts of kindness that often have the most lasting impact. Here are some simple yet powerful ways to cultivate kindness within your family:

1. **Practice Active Listening:** One of the most profound ways to show kindness is by truly listening to each other. In our busy lives, we often hear but don't really listen. Make it a habit to put down your phone, turn off the TV, and give your full attention when a family member is speaking. Show interest in what they have to say, ask questions, and validate their feelings. This small act of being present can make a huge difference,

especially for children who thrive on attention and understanding.

2. **Express Appreciation Regularly:** Words of affirmation are like sunshine for the soul. Make it a point to express gratitude and appreciation daily. This could be as simple as thanking your spouse for making dinner, complimenting your child's artwork, or acknowledging your parent's wisdom. When family members feel appreciated, it fosters a positive environment where kindness can flourish.

3. **Create Family Traditions of Kindness:** Establishing family traditions centered around kindness can be a fun and meaningful way to reinforce this value. Perhaps it's a weekly "kindness night" where each person shares something kind they did that week, or a monthly family volunteering day at a local charity. These traditions can help family members bond while instilling a sense of purpose and gratitude.

4. **Model Kindness in Conflict:** Disagreements and conflicts are a natural part of family life. However, it's how we handle these moments that can either build or break the foundation of kindness. When conflicts arise, practice responding with calmness and empathy instead of anger or frustration. Use "I" statements to express how you feel without blaming others, and encourage open dialogue to find solutions together. By modeling kindness during conflicts, you teach your family how to navigate

differences with respect and compassion.

5. **Express Physical Affection:** Touch is a powerful way to communicate love and kindness. A warm hug, a gentle pat on the back, or even holding hands can create feelings of comfort, security, and connection. Never underestimate the power of a simple touch to express your love and support, especially in challenging times.

6. **Encourage Acts of Service:** Kindness is not just a feeling but an action. Encourage family members to perform acts of service for one another. This could be helping with chores, making a cup of tea for a tired parent, or offering to babysit a sibling's child. Acts of service build empathy and a sense of togetherness that can strengthen family bonds.

7. **Embrace Forgiveness:** Mistakes and misunderstandings are a natural part of any family, but our response to them is what truly counts. Forgive people who have wronged you and give them a second chance. Remember that forgiveness doesn't mean condoning hurtful behavior; it's about choosing to move forward with compassion and understanding. When family members see forgiveness in action, they learn the importance of grace and mercy in their own relationships.

8. **Celebrate Each Other's Successes:** Make it a habit to celebrate the achievements of your family members, no matter how small. Whether it's a good grade on a test, a promotion at work, or learning

a new skill, acknowledging these moments creates a positive environment where everyone feels valued and supported.

The Benefits of a Kind Family Environment

When kindness becomes a natural part of family life, it creates an atmosphere where everyone feels safe, respected, and loved. This kind of environment has numerous benefits:

- **Enhanced Emotional Well-Being:** A kind home is a safe environment where emotions can be openly expressed without fear of judgment. This leads to healthier emotional development in children and reduces stress and anxiety in adults.

- **Stronger Relationships:** Kindness builds trust and deepens connections among family members. When we know we are cared for and valued, we are more likely to open up, communicate honestly, and support one another.

- **Positive Role Modeling:** Children learn by watching the adults around them. When they see their parents and caregivers practicing kindness, they are more likely to adopt those behaviors themselves. This creates a cycle of kindness that continues through generations.

- **Resilience During Tough Times:** A foundation of kindness provides a strong support system during difficult times. Whether facing a family crisis, health issues, or external stressors, families rooted in kindness are better equipped to navigate challenges together.

Building a Legacy of Kindness

Every family has the opportunity to create a unique legacy of kindness. This legacy isn't about perfection; it's about making a conscious choice every day to be more understanding, patient, and compassionate with those we love most. It's about recognizing that every act of kindness, no matter how small, contributes to a larger culture of love and support that benefits everyone.

Call to Action: Start Today

Creating a kind family environment doesn't require a grand overhaul—just a few small steps in the right direction. Start by choosing one simple act of kindness to practice at home this week. Maybe it's committing to active listening during dinner, writing a heartfelt note of appreciation, or planning a family kindness activity.

Remember, kindness is contagious. The more you practice it, the more it will spread throughout your family and beyond. By choosing kindness at home, you are not only enriching your own life but also building a foundation of love and compassion that will support your family for years to come.

So, let's begin today. Let's make kindness a daily habit in our homes, and watch how it transforms our relationships, our families, and ultimately, the world.

CHAPTER 10

Acts of Kindness at Work: Fueling a Positive Culture

Work is a place where most of us spend a large part of our lives. It's where we meet challenges, collaborate with others, and aim to achieve our professional goals. But it can also be a source of stress, competition, and conflict. So, how do we make our workplaces more enjoyable and supportive? The answer is simple: kindness.

Kindness in the workplace is often underestimated, but its impact can be transformative. When people feel valued and respected, they are more engaged, motivated, and productive. A positive workplace culture, fueled by small acts of kindness, not only improves morale but also drives creativity and innovation. Imagine a workplace where people genuinely care about each other's well-being and success—a place where small gestures of kindness make a big difference.

The Power of Small Acts of Kindness at Work

You might think that acts of kindness need to be grand or elaborate to make a real impact, but that couldn't be further from the truth. Small, consistent actions are the ones that truly count. Here are some simple but powerful ways to practice kindness at work:

1. **Offer Genuine Praise and Appreciation**: Recognize a colleague's hard work and efforts. A sincere "thank you" or a compliment on a job well done can boost someone's confidence and motivation. Instead of thinking, "They know I appreciate them," say it out loud. It can turn an average day into a great one.

2. **Lend a Helping Hand**: If you notice a colleague struggling with a task, offer your assistance. Even a small gesture, like holding the door open when their hands are full or helping them carry their coffee, can show that you care. If a co-worker is swamped with deadlines, ask if there's something you can do to lighten their load.

3. **Listen Actively**: In a busy workplace, it's easy to become absorbed in our own to-do lists. But taking a moment to truly listen when a colleague speaks can make them feel valued. Whether it's a work-related issue or something personal, listen with empathy, and show you are genuinely interested in what they have to say.

4. Share Credit and Celebrate Wins: When working in a team, it's essential to acknowledge everyone's contributions. If you're given credit for a project, make sure to highlight the efforts of those who helped you. Celebrating small wins together builds a sense of community and strengthens bonds.

5. Spread Positivity: Start meetings with a positive note or a brief round of gratitude. Share good news, celebrate birthdays, or recognize someone's milestone. Bringing positivity into the room sets the tone for a kinder, more inclusive environment.

Creating a Culture of Kindness at Work

Kindness is contagious. When you initiate acts of kindness at work, you inspire others to do the same. But how do you create a culture where kindness is part of the everyday routine, not just an occasional gesture? Here are some practical ways:

1. **Lead by Example**: Whether you're in a leadership role or not, your behavior sets the tone for others. When you demonstrate kindness, you create a ripple effect. Be the person who greets others with a smile, shows patience in stressful situations, and is always ready to lend a hand.

2. **Foster Open Communication**: Build an environment where people feel at ease sharing their needs and concerns. When people know they can speak openly without judgment, they

are more likely to feel supported and less stressed.

3. **Support Work-Life Balance**: Understand that your colleagues have lives outside of work. Encourage a healthy balance by respecting their time, not sending late-night emails, and being flexible when personal needs arise.

4. **Organize Acts of Kindness Initiatives**: Think about launching a workplace kindness challenge or setting up a "kindness board" where employees can share notes of appreciation and encouragement.This could be as simple as a virtual board in a shared digital workspace or a physical one in the break room.

The Benefits of Kindness at Work

So, what happens when kindness becomes the norm rather than the exception in your workplace? The benefits are numerous:

1. **Increased Employee Satisfaction**: A positive work environment makes people feel happier and more satisfied with their jobs. When employees feel valued and respected, they are more likely to remain loyal and engaged.

2. **Improved Teamwork and Collaboration**: Kindness fosters trust and open communication. Teams that work in an environment of mutual respect and support are more cohesive and effective. They can

share ideas more freely, provide constructive feedback, and support each other in achieving common goals.

3. **Reduced Stress and Burnout**: Kindness can help to alleviate workplace stress. When people feel supported and valued, they are less likely to experience burnout. A kind word or gesture can make a stressful day more manageable.

4. **Enhanced Creativity and Innovation**: A kind workplace encourages risk-taking and innovation. Employees who feel safe are more likely to come up with creative solutions and share them with others. They know they won't be harshly judged if their ideas don't work out.

Overcoming Barriers to Kindness

Of course, there are challenges to cultivating kindness at work. Some may fear that kindness will be perceived as weakness, or they may be concerned about being taken advantage of. It's important to remember that kindness doesn't mean being a pushover; it means being compassionate while still maintaining boundaries.

Here are some tips to overcome common barriers:

1. **Set Clear Boundaries**: Kindness doesn't mean saying "yes" to everything. It's okay to decline requests if you're overloaded or to assertively communicate your needs. Being kind to yourself is also essential.

2. **Stay Genuine**: Kindness should come from a place of sincerity. Don't perform acts of kindness with the expectation of receiving something in return. Authenticity will always resonate more with others.

3. **Address Negative Behavior Constructively**: When faced with unkind behavior, address it calmly and constructively. Approach the person with empathy, expressing how their actions affected you, and offering a solution for moving forward positively.

Call to Action: Be the Spark of Kindness

Acts of kindness are the fuel that powers a positive workplace culture. Start today by choosing one small act of kindness to bring to your workplace. Maybe it's a simple thank you, a genuine compliment, or offering help to a colleague. Remember, every small gesture has the power to create a ripple effect, spreading positivity and transforming your work environment for the better.

Your challenge: Make a commitment to practice at least one act of kindness at work each day for the next week. Observe how these small changes impact not only your mood but also the atmosphere around you. Be the spark that lights the flame of kindness in your workplace, and watch as it grows into a powerful force for good.

CHAPTER 11

Respect at Every Turn: Appreciating Service Workers

Think about the last time you grabbed a cup of coffee, filled your car with gas, or checked out at the grocery store. Each of these moments likely involved a person in the service industry—a barista, a cashier, an attendant—playing a small yet vital role in your day. These workers often go unnoticed, their contributions taken for granted in the rush of daily life. But what if we chose to see them differently? What if we made it a point to show them kindness, to appreciate their work, and to acknowledge their presence in a meaningful way?

The Invisible Workforce

Service workers are everywhere—at the restaurants where we dine, the hotels where we stay, the stores where we shop. They simplify our lives, make them more comfortable, and add to our enjoyment, yet they are often overlooked. Many of these jobs are demanding, requiring long hours on their feet, dealing with challenging customers, and performing repetitive tasks, all while maintaining a cheerful attitude. Despite the importance of their roles, service workers are frequently underpaid, undervalued, and treated as invisible.

So why does it matter if we show kindness to those who serve us? Because kindness has the power to transform these everyday interactions into moments of genuine human connection. When we choose to be kind to service workers, we remind them—and ourselves—of their inherent worth and dignity.

A Simple "Thank You" Goes a Long Way

The simplest way to show kindness to service workers is to say "thank you." It seems obvious, yet it's often forgotten in the haste of our busy lives. Taking a moment to offer a sincere "thank you" can brighten someone's day, make them feel seen, and acknowledge their hard work. It's a small gesture, but it carries immense value. Think about how you feel when someone takes the time to express gratitude for something you've done. It feels good, right? It's the same for service workers. A genuine thank you can be a bright spot in an otherwise tough day.

Look Them in the Eye and Smile

It's so easy to rush through our interactions with service workers—hand over the cash, swipe the card, grab the receipt, and move on without a second thought. But what if, instead, we slowed down just a little? What if we took the time to look them in the eye, smile, and offer a few kind words?

These tiny acts of kindness can make a huge difference. A smile is a universal gesture of goodwill and warmth; it transcends language and cultural barriers. It's a way of saying, "I see you, and I appreciate you." By taking a moment to smile and make eye contact, you're acknowledging the person behind the service, reminding them—and yourself— that they matter.

Acknowledge Their Efforts

Service workers often go above and beyond to ensure we have a pleasant experience, yet these efforts can go unnoticed. When a waiter refills your water without being asked, when a cashier handles a complicated return with patience, or when a hotel staff member remembers your name—these are moments that deserve recognition.

Instead of letting these moments pass by, acknowledge them. A simple comment like, "I really appreciate how attentive you've been," or "Thank you for your patience," can make someone feel valued and respected. When people feel acknowledged for their efforts, it can lift their spirits and foster a positive atmosphere for both the service worker and the customer.

Practice Patience

We've all been there—waiting in line at a busy coffee shop, standing in a slow-moving checkout line, or dealing with a delayed order. It's easy to get frustrated or impatient in these situations, but it's important to remember that the person serving you is often doing their best under challenging circumstances. Instead of letting impatience take over, try practicing patience. Take a deep breath, remind yourself that everyone has bad days, and extend grace to those who might be struggling. Your patience can be a form of kindness that helps ease their stress and make the interaction more pleasant for both of you.

Tip Generously When You Can

If you have the means, tipping generously is a great way to show appreciation for good service. For many service workers, tips make up a significant portion of their income. A few extra dollars might not seem like much to you, but it can make a big difference in someone else's day. And remember, tipping isn't just about the amount; it's also about the intention. Even if you can only afford a small tip, leaving it with a note of thanks or a kind word can leave a lasting impression.

Speak Up for Them

Being kind to service workers also means advocating for them when needed. If you witness someone being mistreated or spoken to disrespectfully, consider speaking up. This doesn't mean escalating a situation, but rather showing support in a calm and respectful way. You could say, "I appreciate how hard you're working," or "I hope you know that you're doing a great job." Your words can serve as a buffer against negativity and show the worker that they are valued and supported.

Learn Their Names and Use Them

One of the most personal ways to show kindness is to learn and use people's names. When you know someone's name, it adds a personal touch to the interaction and makes them feel recognized as an individual rather than just a faceless worker. The next time you frequent your local coffee shop, grocery store, or restaurant, take a moment to learn the names of the people who serve you regularly. A simple "Thank you, Maria" or "I appreciate it, Jason" can go a long way in building a connection and making someone feel special.

Understand Their Perspective

Service workers often deal with situations that can be stressful or challenging, from handling difficult customers to juggling multiple tasks at once. Try to put yourself in their shoes. Imagine what it must be like to stand on your feet for hours or manage demanding clients without a break. Understanding their perspective can help you develop empathy, which naturally leads to kinder interactions.

Create Moments of Joy

Sometimes, being kind means going the extra mile

to create moments of joy for others. Leave a positive review mentioning the person by name, bring in a small treat for the staff, or simply compliment them on a job well done. These gestures can create memorable moments that brighten a person's day and foster a culture of kindness that spreads beyond just you and them.

Call to Action: Make Kindness a Daily Habit

The next time you encounter a service worker—whether at a store, restaurant, or anywhere else—take a moment to consciously practice kindness. Say thank you, smile, ask how their day is going, or find another small way to show appreciation.

Make it a habit to notice the people who serve you and acknowledge their efforts. Your kindness can turn a routine transaction into a positive, uplifting experience for both of you.

Remember, kindness is contagious. The more you practice it, the more it spreads, creating ripples that reach far beyond what you might ever know. Let's choose to be kind at every turn, starting with the people who make our daily lives a little easier. Will you take this small but powerful step today?

CHAPTER 12

Navigating the Online World with Grace

The internet is a vast and incredible place, a digital wonderland where information flows freely, ideas are exchanged in real-time, and people from all corners of the world can connect with one another. It can be a tool for learning, a platform for sharing creativity, or a means of keeping in touch with loved ones. Yet, as with any space we inhabit, the online world can be as cold and unfriendly as it is captivating. Often, the screen creates a sense of distance that makes it easy to forget there are real people behind those usernames and profile pictures—people with emotions, stories, and feelings.

This distance can lead to misunderstandings, conflicts, or even cruelty, turning the digital world into a place of hostility. But just as kindness can transform our real-world interactions, it has the power to make our online experiences more meaningful, compassionate, and human.

So, how can we show kindness in a place where the usual cues—tone of voice, facial expressions, body language—are absent? Let's explore practical ways to cultivate "digital decency" and show kindness in our online interactions.

1. Pause Before You Post

One of the simplest, yet most profound, ways to practice kindness online is to take a moment to pause before hitting that "send" or "post" button. The internet's anonymity can occasionally cause people to behave at their worst. making it easier to say things we wouldn't dream of saying face-to-face. Pausing gives us a moment to consider how our words might be received.

Ask yourself: Is this comment constructive or helpful? Could it be misinterpreted as hurtful or dismissive? Taking a moment to pause and reflect can prevent impulsive reactions that might cause unnecessary pain or conflict.

2. Be Generous with Your Encouragement

The internet has led to the emergence of numerous platforms where people share their thoughts, creativity, and life experiences. From a friend's social media post about their new project to a stranger's heartfelt story on a forum, there are endless opportunities to uplift others with simple, kind words.

Leaving a positive comment, sharing someone's work, or simply clicking "like" can mean the world to someone. Think of how a small act of kindness, like a compliment from a friend or a word of encouragement, can brighten your day. Why not pass that feeling on to someone else?

3. Resist the Urge to Engage in Arguments

It's easy to get drawn into online debates, especially when you feel passionately about a topic. But sometimes, what starts as a discussion quickly escalates into an argument, where both sides are more interested in "winning" than understanding one another.

Instead of jumping into an argument, consider approaching disagreements with curiosity and empathy. Try to understand where the other person is coming from and acknowledge their point of view, even if you don't agree. A simple, "I see your perspective; here's mine" can go a long way in keeping the conversation respectful and productive. Remember, it's okay to disengage from conversations that are becoming toxic or unkind.

4. Practice Empathy

Empathy is the foundation of kindness, whether online or offline. It's the ability to put ourselves in another person's shoes and consider their feelings and experiences. In the digital world, empathy means remembering that the person on the other side of the screen is human, just like you.

If someone makes a mistake, instead of rushing to criticize, consider how you would feel if you were in their position. If someone seems rude or aggressive, remember that you don't know what they might be going through. Offering a little grace and understanding can go a long way in creating a kinder online environment.

5. Share Information Thoughtfully

Misinformation spreads like wildfire online. Before sharing that article, meme, or piece of news, take a moment to verify its accuracy. Spreading false information, even unintentionally, can cause harm, panic, or confusion.

Kindness online also means being a responsible sharer of information. If you come across misinformation, approach it gently. Instead of attacking the person who shared it, provide a credible source or fact-checking link and kindly explain why the information might not be accurate. This approach fosters understanding rather than defensiveness.

6. Acknowledge Mistakes and Apologize

We all make mistakes, and online, they can feel amplified due to the sheer number of people who might see them. If you realize you've made an error, whether it's a misunderstanding, a wrong fact, or an unkind comment, own up to it and apologize sincerely. A sincere apology can significantly help mend relationships and show integrity.

An apology might look like, "I realize my comment may have come across as harsh, and that wasn't my intention. I'm sorry if it hurt you." This simple acknowledgment of a mistake can open the door to healing and understanding.

7. Use Humor Wisely

Humor can be a great way to build a connection. but it's important to use it thoughtfully. Sarcasm, jokes, or comments that might seem funny in person can easily be misinterpreted in writing. When using humor, consider the context and the people involved. If there's any doubt that your joke might be taken the wrong way, it's better to err on the side of caution.

8. Practice Digital Mindfulness

Our online presence greatly influences our mental

well-being. Engaging in toxic interactions, doom-scrolling, or consuming negative content can leave us feeling drained, anxious, or even angry. Practicing digital mindfulness means being intentional about how we spend our time online. It involves setting boundaries, taking breaks, and choosing to engage in positive, uplifting content.

Consider setting a specific time each day to unplug and reconnect with the physical world. Take this opportunity to rest, contemplate, and participate in activities that make you happy. This break can help you return to the digital space with a refreshed perspective, ready to contribute kindness and positivity.

9. Protect Your Privacy and That of Others

Respecting privacy is an often overlooked but critical aspect of online kindness. Avoid sharing private messages, personal information, or photos of others without their consent. Protecting the privacy of yourself and others shows respect and consideration for people's boundaries and personal lives.

Call to Action: Become a Digital Ambassador of Kindness

Now, let's make a commitment together. The next time you're online, make a conscious effort to be kinder. Whether that means pausing before you post, sharing an encouraging word, or simply showing empathy toward someone who might need it, remember that every act of kindness counts.

Challenge yourself to do one kind thing online each day. It could be as simple as sending a supportive message to a friend, offering a word of comfort to someone who's struggling, or choosing not to engage in a negative conversation. Imagine if we all made this small effort—how much brighter and kinder our digital world would be!

The online world is what we make of it. Let's fill it with kindness, one post, comment, and click at a time.

CHAPTER 13

Bridging Divides: The Power of Kindness in Politics

Politics often feels like a battleground—a space where debates can turn heated, disagreements become personal, and where the loudest voices often drown out the quieter, more thoughtful ones. The mere mention of politics can make many of us feel tense, angry, or even hopeless. It's easy to think that kindness and politics don't mix, that in a world so polarized, kindness might be seen as a sign of weakness or naivety. But what if kindness could be the key to bridging the divides we see today?

Kindness in politics isn't about ignoring the issues or pretending that differences don't exist. It's about approaching these differences with an open heart and a willingness to listen and understand. It's about finding common ground and showing respect, even when we don't agree. Let's explore how kindness can transform the political landscape, one conversation at a time.

Why Kindness Matters in Politics

Politics is about people, and where there are people, there are emotions, needs, and stories. Every person who enters a political debate, whether it's on the global stage or over a dinner table, brings with them their experiences, values, and beliefs. When we focus only on winning an argument, we often forget that there's a human being on the other side of the discussion.

Kindness in politics matters because it humanizes these interactions. It reminds us that behind every opinion is a person who, just like us, wants to be heard and understood. When we approach political conversations with kindness, we're more likely to build trust, open up dialogue, and find solutions that benefit everyone. Kindness doesn't mean compromising your values or giving up on what you believe is right; it means advocating for those beliefs with empathy and respect.

Real-Life Examples of Kindness in Politics

Kindness in politics isn't just a lofty ideal; it's something that has been demonstrated in real life, often with powerful results.

1. John McCain and Barack Obama: Mutual Respect Across the Aisle

Consider the relationship between the late Senator

John McCain, a Republican, and former President Barack Obama, a Democrat. Despite their political differences, both men demonstrated mutual respect and kindness towards each other. When McCain ran against Obama in the 2008 presidential election, the campaign was heated, but McCain was known for defending Obama's character, even when his supporters tried to attack it. At a rally, when a woman falsely claimed Obama was an Arab, McCain calmly corrected her, saying, "No, ma'am, he's a decent family man and citizen."

This act of kindness did not mean McCain agreed with Obama's policies; it meant he respected him as a person. Their relationship showed that it's possible to hold strong political beliefs while also treating opponents with decency and respect.

2. The Story of Ruth Bader Ginsburg and Antonin Scalia: A Friendship Beyond Disagreements

Another example is the unlikely friendship between U.S. Supreme Court Justices Ruth Bader Ginsburg and Antonin Scalia. They were known for having vastly different judicial philosophies—Ginsburg was a liberal icon, while Scalia was a staunch conservative. Yet, they shared a deep friendship that was built on mutual respect and admiration.

They often dined together, attended the opera, and even vacationed together. Ginsburg once said that Scalia made her a better justice by challenging her views, forcing her to think more deeply and articulate her arguments more clearly. Their friendship didn't diminish their differences; it enriched them. Their example shows that kindness and civility can coexist with profound disagreement, leading to a more productive and respectful dialogue.

Practical Ways to Show Kindness in Politics

So, how can we bring kindness into political conversations in our daily lives? Here are some practical strategies:

1. Listen to Understand, Not to Respond

One of the biggest challenges in political discussions is that we often listen with the intent to reply, not to understand. The next time you find yourself in a heated debate, try to listen fully before jumping in with your own point of view. Ask questions to clarify the other person's position, and show genuine curiosity about their perspective. This doesn't mean you have to agree with them, but it demonstrates respect and opens the door to a more meaningful conversation.

2. Avoid Personal Attacks

It's easy to get emotional when talking about politics, but personal attacks only escalate tension and shut down productive dialogue. Instead of saying, "You're wrong" or "You don't know what you're talking about," focus on the issue at hand. Use "I" statements to express how you feel about the topic, such as, "I see it differently because…" or "I believe that…". This approach helps keep the conversation respectful and focused on the ideas, not the individual.

3. Find Common Ground

No matter how divided we might seem, there's usually some common ground to be found. It might be a shared concern for the environment, a desire for better education, or a passion for social justice. By finding these areas of agreement, you create a foundation for a more constructive conversation. Start by acknowledging the points where you both agree, and then build from there. For example, you might say, "We both want what's best for our community, even if we have different ideas on how to achieve it."

4. Share Personal Stories

Politics can often feel abstract, but sharing personal stories can make it more relatable and less adversarial. Instead of just citing statistics or policies, talk about why a particular issue matters to you personally. Maybe you're passionate about healthcare because a loved one struggled to get the care they needed. Sharing your story can create empathy and understanding, even if the other person doesn't agree with your stance.

5. Practice Gratitude and Grace

When someone takes the time to engage in a political conversation with you, even if it gets heated, express gratitude for their willingness to discuss the issue. You might say, "Thank you for sharing your perspective" or "I appreciate you taking the time to talk about this." This simple act can defuse tension and create a more respectful atmosphere.

The Multiplier Effect of Kindness in Politics

When we bring kindness into political conversations, it doesn't just affect the immediate discussion; it can have a multiplier effect. Imagine a world where more people approached political differences with kindness —where debates were more about finding solutions than winning arguments, where empathy and respect were the norms, not the exceptions.

Kindness in politics might seem like a small gesture, but it can inspire others to do the same. When we model respectful and kind behavior, we set an example for others to follow. And slowly, conversation by conversation, we can help create a political climate that values understanding over division, connection over conflict.

Your Call to Action

This week, challenge yourself to bring kindness into at least one political conversation. Whether it's with a friend, a colleague, or even a stranger online, try to practice one of the strategies we've discussed. Remember, kindness doesn't mean avoiding tough topics or pretending to agree. It means approaching these topics with respect, empathy, and a genuine desire to understand.

By doing so, you'll be helping to build bridges instead of walls, fostering a sense of connection even in the midst of disagreement. And who knows? Your small act of kindness could be the spark that inspires others to do the same. After all, kindness is powerful, even in politics.

CHAPTER 14
Being Kind to the Planet: Kindness Toward the Environment

When we think about kindness, we often think of how we treat the people around us—our family, friends, colleagues, or even strangers. But what about our kindness toward the world we live in? The earth, after all, is our shared home, and just like any good home, it requires care and respect to remain a place where we can thrive. Acts of kindness toward the environment may not always be as obvious as a smile or a compliment, but they are just as meaningful. In fact, they are acts that can ripple outward, touching countless lives and generations yet to come.

Kindness to the planet isn't about grand gestures or radical changes. It's about small, mindful actions that make a difference over time. Just like being kind to others involves thoughtfulness and empathy, so does being kind to the earth. It begins with a shift in perspective—from seeing the environment as something separate from ourselves to recognizing it as an integral part of our daily lives.

The Power of Small Actions

It's easy to feel overwhelmed by the enormity of environmental issues. Climate change, pollution, deforestation—these problems seem too vast for any one person to tackle. But here's the thing: change starts with small, simple actions. Consider the story of a person who begins by picking up a piece of litter on the sidewalk. That single act, seemingly insignificant, can inspire others who witness it to do the same. Before long, an entire community might be moved to keep their surroundings clean. The same concept applies to acts of kindness toward the planet.

Start with something small. Maybe it's deciding to bring a reusable bag to the grocery store or choosing to walk or bike instead of driving your car for short trips. These decisions might feel trivial in isolation, but multiplied by millions of people, they add up to a profound impact. The truth is, small changes can create a powerful wave of positive action.

Mindful Consumption: Reducing Waste

One of the most impactful ways to show kindness to the planet is to be mindful of our consumption. Every product we buy has a life cycle—from the resources used to make it to the waste it becomes when we're done with it. By making more thoughtful choices about what we purchase, we can reduce the amount of waste we produce.

Consider adopting a "reduce, reuse, recycle" mindset. Reducing starts with questioning whether you really need something before you buy it. Could you borrow it from a friend, rent it, or perhaps find it second-hand? Reusing involves finding new purposes for items rather than throwing them away. That old glass jar might make a perfect container for pantry staples, or those worn-out jeans could become a trendy tote bag. Finally, recycling ensures that materials like plastic, paper, and metal are processed and reused, rather than ending up in landfills.

But mindful consumption isn't just about material goods; it extends to energy use as well. Simple things like turning off lights when you exit a room, unplugging devices that aren't in use, or lowering the thermostat by a degree or two can significantly reduce your energy footprint. It may seem like a small effort, but when these habits become routine, they contribute to a more sustainable world.

Nurturing Green Spaces

Another meaningful way to show kindness to our planet is to nurture green spaces. Whether it's planting a tree, tending to a community garden, or simply caring for the plants in your own backyard, these actions can have a big impact. Trees and plants provide essential services—they clean the air, regulate temperatures, provide habitats for wildlife, and even improve our mental health.

If you have a small garden, consider planting native species that need less water and maintenance. If you don't have a garden, look for opportunities to volunteer in community gardening projects or participate in local tree-planting initiatives. Even planting a single tree or cultivating a few flowers on a balcony can contribute to a healthier environment. Remember, every plant matters in the fight against climate change.

Conscious Eating: Choosing Plant-Based Options

Did you know that the way we eat can also be an act of kindness toward the planet? What we choose to eat can have a significant impact on the environment, especially when it comes to meat and dairy production, which are major contributors to greenhouse gas emissions, deforestation, and water consumption.

You don't have to become a vegetarian or vegan overnight to make a difference. Start by putting more plant-based meals into your daily diet—perhaps one day a week, like the popular "Meatless Monday" initiative. You might find that experimenting with new recipes and flavors is a fun way to explore new foods and reduce your environmental footprint.

Supporting Sustainable Practices

Being kind to the planet also means supporting businesses and practices that prioritize sustainability. This could mean choosing products that are certified organic, fair trade, or produced by companies committed to reducing their environmental impact. Whenever possible, buy local. Local goods not only support the economy in your community, but they also reduce the carbon footprint linked to the transportation of goods over long distances.

Another way to support sustainable practices is to voice your concerns. Contact local representatives about environmental issues or join groups and organizations that are advocating for sustainable practices and policies. Our voices, collectively, can drive change at a systemic level.

Practicing Digital Decluttering

In today's digital age, our online habits also have an environmental impact. Every email we send, photo we upload, or video we stream requires energy, usually in the form of electricity from data centers. Digital decluttering is a simple way to reduce your digital carbon footprint. Start by cleaning out your email inbox, deleting old files and photos you no longer need, and unsubscribing from newsletters you don't read. You might be surprised at how these small acts can lighten your digital load and benefit the planet.

Teaching and Inspiring Others

Perhaps one of the most powerful acts of kindness you can do for the planet is to share what you've learned with others. When you inspire those around you to make more eco-friendly choices, you're multiplying the impact of your efforts. Host a workshop, start a book club with an environmental focus, or simply talk to friends and family about the changes you're making and why. Sometimes, a heartfelt conversation is all it takes to spark meaningful change.

Call to Action: One Kind Act at a Time

Now that you have a few ideas, I invite you to take the first step. Pick just one act of kindness toward the planet and make it a habit this week. Whether it's bringing a reusable cup to your favorite coffee shop, starting a compost pile in your backyard, or choosing a plant-based meal, each small decision makes a difference.

Remember, kindness to the planet is kindness to ourselves, our neighbors, and future generations. Let's make a conscious effort to show kindness to our environment, one step at a time. As you do, you'll not only help create a healthier planet, but you'll also find a deeper connection to the world around you—one that fosters gratitude, joy, and purpose. So, go ahead —be kind to the earth, and watch how it transforms your life and the lives of others in ways you never imagined.

CHAPTER 15
How Caring for Other Species Enriches Our Lives

When we talk about kindness, we often focus on how we treat other people. But what about our relationship with the animals that share our world? Animals are more than just background characters in our human stories; they are sentient beings who experience joy, fear, love, and pain. By extending kindness to animals, we not only help them, but we also enrich our own lives in surprising and meaningful ways.

Showing kindness to animals can be as simple as offering a friendly gesture to a stray cat, volunteering at a local shelter, or choosing cruelty-free products. These acts may seem small, but they have a powerful impact on both the animals we care for and our own sense of well-being. Let's explore why kindness to animals matters and how it can lead to a richer, more compassionate life.

The Connection Between Humans and Animals

A unique bond between humans and animals has endured for thousands of years. From the earliest domestication of dogs and cats to the complex relationships we have with pets, farm animals, and wildlife today, animals have always played a significant role in our lives. They offer companionship, teach us about empathy and patience, and remind us of the beauty and simplicity of the natural world.

Research has demonstrated that interacting with animals can have a positive impact on both our mental and physical health. For example, petting a dog can lower blood pressure, reduce stress, and boost levels of serotonin and dopamine—the "feel-good" chemicals in our brains. Beyond the physical benefits, there's something deeply soul-nourishing about connecting with another living creature, especially one that relies on us for care and companionship.

Acts of Kindness Toward Animals

So, how do we go about being kinder to the animals around us? It starts with awareness and a genuine desire to make a difference, no matter how small. Here are a few ways you can practice kindness toward animals in your everyday life:

1. **Adopt, Don't Shop:** One of the most direct ways to show kindness to animals is by adopting a pet from a shelter rather than purchasing one from a breeder or pet store. By adopting, you're giving a second chance to an animal that may have faced hardship

or abandonment. If adoption isn't an option for you, consider fostering. Fostering an animal can help shelters create more space and allow you to make a positive impact without a long-term commitment.

2. **Volunteer Your Time:** Many animal shelters and rescue organizations rely heavily on volunteers. Donating your time to walk dogs, play with cats, clean enclosures, or help with adoption events can make a huge difference. Not only will you be supporting the animals, but you'll also be supporting your community and connecting with others who share your passion for animal welfare.

3. **Practice Compassionate Consumerism:** Our purchasing choices can greatly influence animal welfare. Look for products that are cruelty-free, meaning they have not been tested on animals. You can find this information on packaging or by researching brands online. Choosing to buy ethically sourced meat, dairy, and eggs—or reducing your consumption of animal products altogether—can also make a big difference. Supporting local farmers who treat their animals humanely is another way to show kindness through your purchases.

4. **Support Wildlife Protection:** Kindness to animals isn't just about our pets—it extends to wildlife as well. One way to help is by supporting conservation efforts. This could mean donating to wildlife organizations, participating in local clean-up projects to protect habitats, or even planting a

wildlife-friendly garden to provide food and shelter for local species. Being mindful of our actions, such as reducing plastic use, can help protect marine animals who are particularly vulnerable to pollution.

5. **Speak Up for Animals:** Animals cannot speak for themselves, so it's up to us to be their voice. Educate yourself about animal welfare issues and advocate for positive change. Whether it's signing petitions, writing to lawmakers about animal protection laws, or sharing information on social media, your voice can help create a more compassionate world for all living creatures.

6. **Practice Everyday Acts of Kindness:** Even small actions can make a big difference. Leave a bowl of fresh water outside for stray animals on hot days, be careful not to disturb wildlife when you're out in nature, and always approach animals with gentleness and respect. These little acts of kindness can brighten an animal's day and build a culture of compassion.

The Impact of Kindness to Animals

Being kind to animals has a profound effect on us. Caring for another creature teaches us empathy, patience, and responsibility. It challenges us to look beyond our needs and see the world from another perspective. Animals live in the moment—they don't hold grudges or worry about the future. They remind us to appreciate the simple things in life and find joy in the present.

When we are kind to animals, we often find ourselves more attuned to the natural world around us. We start noticing the song of a bird, the way a squirrel plays in a tree, or the curious look of a neighborhood cat. This awareness can foster a deeper sense of gratitude and connection to life as a whole.

Kindness to animals also fosters a sense of purpose. Whether you're caring for a beloved pet or advocating for wildlife conservation, knowing that you are making a positive difference can give your life meaning and direction. It allows us to step outside ourselves and be part of something bigger.

A Kinder World for All

Imagine a world where kindness toward animals is a given—a world where no animal suffers from neglect, abuse, or abandonment. This vision starts with each of us making small changes in our daily lives. The positive effect of these acts of kindness can be far-reaching, impacting not just animals but our own sense of happiness and fulfillment.

Call to Action: Make a Commitment

Now that you have some ideas on how to be kinder to animals, it's time to take action. Choose one act of kindness to start with this week. Maybe you decide to donate to a local animal shelter, volunteer an hour of your time, or make a conscious effort to buy cruelty-free products. Whatever it is, make a commitment to be more mindful of the animals around you.

Remember, kindness is not just something we do; it's a way of being. When we show kindness to animals, we cultivate a more compassionate heart, open ourselves up to deeper connections, and enrich our lives in ways we never thought possible. So go ahead—extend a hand, a voice, or a heart to the animals in your life, and watch how it transforms your world.

CHAPTER 16
Don't Keep A Kindness Ledger

Imagine for a moment that kindness is like an endless, flowing river. When we dip our hands into it, we can't measure the water that passes through our fingers. We just enjoy the cool sensation and know there's always more to come. But what happens if we try to bottle that water and keep track of every drop? Suddenly, something so pure and refreshing becomes complicated, heavy, and burdensome.

This is what happens when we keep a "kindness ledger" — when we mentally note every favor, every good deed, and every nice thing someone has done for us, or we've done for them, like we're accountants of our relationships. We start thinking in terms of "I owe you one" or "They owe me." But kindness isn't a transaction; it's a gift, and it loses its magic when we treat it like a business deal.

The Trouble with Keeping Score

Think back to a time when someone did something nice for you — maybe a friend paid for your coffee, or a colleague covered for you at work. It felt good, right? But what if that same person later reminded you of that favor, subtly or not-so-subtly hinting that it's your turn to return the gesture? Suddenly, that simple act of kindness feels like a debt hanging over your head. It no longer feels like a gift but an obligation. The warm feeling you initially had gets replaced by a sense of pressure or even resentment.

Keeping a kindness ledger can harm our relationships in more ways than one. When we constantly tally up the favors and good deeds, we turn what should be an act of love or friendship into a cold, calculated exchange. We may start feeling resentful if we think we're giving more than we're receiving. On the other hand, if we're always worried about what we "owe" someone, we might stop ourselves from genuinely enjoying their kindness. In both cases, the natural flow of giving and receiving is disrupted, replaced by a tense, uncomfortable balance sheet.

The Freedom of Letting Go

Letting go of the need to keep score is liberating. It allows us to be more spontaneous and genuine with our kindness, without the weight of expectations dragging us down. When we're not keeping track, we're free to act out of love, compassion, or simply because we want to — not because we feel we have to.

Consider the example of Maya, a single mom who

lives in a tight-knit community. Maya often helps her elderly neighbor, Mrs. Thompson, by picking up groceries, mowing the lawn, or just sitting down for a chat. She does it without a second thought, without keeping track of how many times she's helped or what Mrs. Thompson has done in return. She knows Mrs. Thompson can't do much for her in a material sense, but Maya doesn't mind. For her, kindness is its own reward.

One day, Maya's car breaks down on her way to work, and she's stuck by the side of the road with her two kids in the backseat. Who shows up to help? Mrs. Thompson's son, who happens to be driving by. He offers to take the kids to school and arranges for a mechanic to fix the car. Maya didn't expect this — she never kept a ledger with Mrs. Thompson. But the kindness she'd given freely came back to her in a different, unexpected way. This is the beauty of not keeping score. When we act out of pure kindness, the goodness often finds its way back to us, in ways we can't foresee.

Practical Advice: How to Break Free from the Kindness Ledger Mentality

1. **Shift Your Perspective**: Remind yourself that kindness is a way of being, not a currency to be traded. It's about who you are, not about what you get in return. Ask yourself, "Am I doing this because I genuinely want to, or because I expect something in return?" If it's the latter, take a step back and

reconsider your motivations.

2. **Practice Gratitude**: Focus on what you have received, not what you're owed. Keep a gratitude journal where you jot down acts of kindness that come your way, without thinking about when or how to repay them. This practice can help shift your mindset from tallying up favors to embracing gratitude.

3. **Give Without Expectation**: Make a conscious effort to do something kind each day with no strings attached. It could be as simple as holding the door for someone, complimenting a stranger, or sending a kind message to a friend. Notice how it feels when you're not looking for anything in return.

4. **Communicate Openly**: If you find yourself feeling burdened by the feeling that you "owe" someone, have an open conversation about it. Sometimes, we build these ledgers in our heads without realizing that the other person doesn't feel the same way. A simple chat can clear the air and prevent misunderstandings.

5. **Embrace Imperfection**: Understand that no relationship will ever be perfectly balanced. Sometimes, you will give more; other times, you will receive more. And that's okay. Accept that imbalance as a natural part of human connections.

Real-Life Example: The Surprise of Unconditional Kindness

A great example of breaking free from the kindness ledger is the story of a man named Kevin. Kevin's best friend, Jason, had always been there for him, helping him move, supporting him during tough times, and always showing up when needed. Kevin felt indebted and worried he could never "repay" Jason for all the kindness he had received.

One day, Kevin decided to talk to Jason about it. Jason laughed and said, "I never thought of it that way. I do those things because I care about you, not because I expect anything back. And guess what? When you showed up at my dad's funeral, even though you had to drive four hours to get there, that meant more to me than any favor I could ever do for you."

Kevin realized that his friendship with Jason wasn't a ledger to be balanced but a mutual exchange of care, love, and support, often in ways that can't be measured or compared. From that day, Kevin stopped keeping score. He learned to appreciate Jason's kindness without the pressure of owing anything back.

The Power of Kindness Without a Ledger

The true power of kindness lies in its unpredictability, its ability to surprise and delight without any strings attached. When we let go of the ledger, we create space for genuine connections. We stop worrying about what's "fair" and start focusing on what feels right. We open ourselves to a world where kindness flows naturally, like that endless river, nourishing our souls and brightening our days.

Call To Action

So, let's challenge ourselves to stop keeping score, to stop measuring our relationships in transactions. Instead, let's give freely, love deeply, and trust that kindness, like water, will always find its way back to us in the most unexpected and beautiful ways.

CHAPTER 17

Mending Hearts: The Power of Forgiveness

Forgiveness. Just the word can stir up a range of emotions—anger, sadness, resentment, or even fear. It's one of those actions that is often easier said than done. But what if I told you that forgiveness is one of the most powerful forms of kindness? Not just kindness toward others, but also toward ourselves.

At its core, forgiveness is about releasing the heavy weight of resentment or anger we carry around when we've been hurt. It's an act that brings freedom and healing, allowing us to mend our hearts and open up to life's goodness once again. In this chapter, we'll explore how forgiveness is a powerful expression of kindness, how it impacts both the forgiver and the forgiven, and how we can start incorporating forgiveness into our daily lives.

The Healing Power of Forgiveness

To truly understand forgiveness, we first need to debunk a few myths. Forgiveness doesn't mean erasing the memory, justifying the wrong, or overlooking what occurred. It's not about letting someone off the hook or pretending that everything is fine when it isn't. Instead, forgiveness is a conscious choice to let go of the grip that a past hurt has on you. It's deciding that the pain of the past will no longer dictate your present or future.

Take the story of Sandra, for example. Sandra had a close friend, Mia, with whom she shared everything —her dreams, her fears, her struggles. They were like sisters, inseparable. But one day, Sandra discovered that Mia had been spreading rumors about her at work, damaging her reputation. The betrayal cut deep. Sandra felt anger, sadness, and confusion. She wanted to confront Mia, to lash out, to make her feel the same pain. But after the initial shock subsided, Sandra realized something important: holding onto that anger wasn't hurting Mia; it was hurting herself.

Sandra chose a different path. She decided to forgive Mia, not for Mia's sake, but for her own peace of mind. She sent a heartfelt message, acknowledging the hurt but also expressing her willingness to let go and move on. To her surprise, Mia responded with sincere regret and an apology. Their friendship didn't return to what it was, but Sandra felt a sense of relief and lightness. She felt empowered by her choice to forgive, a decision that allowed her to mend her heart and focus on her own happiness.

Why Forgiveness is a Kindness—To Others and Ourselves

Forgiveness is like a bridge—it connects our past selves, who were hurt, to our future selves, who deserve peace. And kindness is the wood and nails that build that bridge. When we forgive, we are extending an olive branch not just to the person who hurt us, but also to ourselves. We are saying, "I deserve to be free of this burden."

Think about it: when you hold onto anger, who does it really affect? Often, the person who hurt you has moved on. They may not even know the extent of your pain. Meanwhile, you're left with sleepless nights, a clenched jaw, or a heavy heart. The act of forgiveness frees you from that trap. It's a gift you give yourself—a chance to breathe easier and live lighter.

A study from the Journal of Behavioral Medicine found that people who forgive tend to have lower blood pressure, reduced anxiety, and a stronger immune system. Forgiveness isn't just an abstract concept—it's a physical release. Your body, heart, and mind all feel the impact.

Real-Life Example of Forgiveness

Consider the story of a woman named Mary Johnson. Her son was murdered, and for years, she was consumed by rage toward his killer. But she found no peace in her anger. Eventually, Mary made the incredible decision to meet the man who had taken her son's life. They sat down, face to face, and talked for hours. Mary felt her heart soften as she listened to his story of remorse and regret. In a moment of profound grace, she chose to forgive him. Today, they share a unique bond, and Mary says that forgiving him was the most freeing and healing thing she ever did.

Practical Steps to Practice Forgiveness

So, how do we move from the idea of forgiveness to the act of forgiving? Here are some practical steps:

1. **Acknowledge Your Feelings**: It's okay to feel hurt, angry, or upset. Give yourself permission to feel your emotions fully. Record them in a journal or share them with a trusted friend. Recognizing your pain is the first step toward healing.**Empathize with the Offender**: This is often the hardest part, but try to see things from the other person's perspective. What might have led them to act the way they did? This doesn't mean you condone their actions, but understanding their humanity can soften your heart.

2. **Make the Choice**: Remember, forgiveness is a choice you make for yourself. It doesn't have to happen overnight. It can be a gradual process, and that's okay. Decide that you will start the journey toward forgiveness, even if you don't feel fully ready.

3. **Communicate if You Can**: If it feels safe and right, consider expressing your feelings to the person who hurt you. This can be in person, through a letter, or

even in a private journal entry that you never send. Sometimes, putting your thoughts into words helps you process and release them.

4. **Focus on Your Growth**: Forgiveness is not just about what happened in the past; it's about what you want for your future. Redirect your energy toward things that bring you joy and growth. This might mean taking up a new hobby, spending time with supportive people, or even seeking professional help if needed.

5. **Practice Self-Kindness**: Forgiveness begins with self-compassion. Be kind to yourself as you navigate your feelings. Understand that forgiving someone doesn't mean you have to forget or pretend it didn't happen. It means you are choosing peace over pain.

The Far-Reaching Power of Forgiveness

When you choose to forgive, you not only heal yourself but also contribute to a broader sense of kindness in the world. Your example can inspire others to practice forgiveness, encouraging them to break the cycle of hurt and begin a journey of understanding and compassion.

Forgiveness has a way of reaching beyond just the immediate situation. Your decision to forgive, to be kind in the face of pain, can touch the lives of others in meaningful and sometimes unexpected ways. By choosing forgiveness, you foster a space where empathy and kindness can flourish, and where others feel encouraged to do the same.

A Call to Action: Start Your Forgiveness Journey Today

Take a moment to think about someone you need to forgive—maybe it's a friend, a family member, or even yourself. And, begin the process of forgiving them. What steps can you take today to start that journey? Remember, forgiveness is a powerful act of kindness that can mend hearts—yours and others.

By choosing to forgive, you are choosing to heal, to grow, and to live a life unburdened by the past. You are choosing kindness, and in doing so, you are transforming not only your own life but the world around you. And remember, forgiveness is not a sign of weakness; it is a testament to your strength. It's a conscious decision to rise above pain and to live with an open heart. The power of forgiveness is in your hands—use it to mend hearts, including your own.

CHAPTER 18
The Quiet Gift: Doing Good Without Being Noticed

Think of a world where every kind deed you do is met with applause, likes, or public praise. Sounds appealing, right? We live in a time where recognition feels like a currency—something to be earned and spent to boost our self-esteem. However, there's a quieter, deeper power in acts of kindness done without any expectation of recognition. This is what I like to call "silent kindness."

Silent kindness isn't about being invisible. It's about choosing to be humble, to do good without a spotlight, and to find joy in the act itself rather than in the validation it might bring. It's the type of kindness that shapes your character, strengthens your empathy, and brings an unspoken connection between you and others. It's kindness for the sake of kindness—pure, simple, and transformative.

The Quiet Magic of Silent Kindness

What makes silent kindness so powerful? It's the unexpected effect it creates. Think of the time you found a note of encouragement left on your car windshield on a hard day, or when someone paid for your coffee in the drive-thru line without leaving their name. Those moments, small as they seem, linger in our minds. They make us feel seen, valued, and uplifted. Silent acts of kindness have a way of touching hearts in a profound way because they come without strings attached, without an expectation of reciprocation or even acknowledgment.

Consider the story of Mary, a schoolteacher in her fifties who often spent her weekends in a small, hidden corner of her community. She visited the local laundromat and left quarters on top of the washing machines, just enough for someone to do a load of laundry. She did this without leaving a note, without any indication of who had left the gift. One day, a friend of hers who had no idea Mary was behind the acts told her how this simple gesture had brought unexpected relief during a particularly tough week. Mary just smiled, and in that moment, she felt the quiet joy that comes from giving without expecting anything in return. That's the beauty of silent kindness—it's a circle that completes itself.

Why Practice Silent Kindness?

When we do something kind without seeking recognition, we tap into a deeper, more genuine part of ourselves. Here are a few reasons why silent kindness is worth embracing:

1. **Builds Genuine Empathy**: When you practice kindness without recognition, you learn to do it for the right reasons. You stop worrying about what others think and start focusing on how your actions make others feel. This shift helps you build authentic empathy, seeing the world through others' eyes and feeling more connected to their experiences.

2. **Reduces the Ego**: Recognition can sometimes inflate our sense of self-worth, attaching it to external validation. Silent kindness, on the other hand, challenges us to find satisfaction internally. It's an exercise in humility, reminding us that we are not the center of the universe. Instead, we are part of a larger human story, and every act of kindness is a thread that binds us closer to one another.

3. **Fosters Inner Joy**: There is a quiet joy in doing something kind that only you know about. It's like having a secret with the universe. It feels special, almost sacred. It's a joy that doesn't fade with time because it's not dependent on a fleeting moment of recognition.

4. **Promotes Selfless Giving**: Silent kindness teaches us to give without strings attached. We learn to let go of expectations—no thank you cards, no social media shout-outs, just pure, selfless giving. This can be liberating and can open us up to more opportunities for spontaneous kindness.

Real-Life Examples of Silent Kindness

Take inspiration from John, a businessman who made a habit of carrying $5 gift cards to a local coffee shop in his wallet. Whenever he saw someone who looked like they were having a hard day—a mother juggling kids, a tired nurse, or a stressed student—he would hand them a card and simply say, "This is for you. I hope your day gets a little brighter." He never lingered for a thank-you or explained himself; he just moved on. John's small, silent gestures brought smiles to countless faces, but what he found was that it also brightened his own life in unexpected ways. He felt more connected to his community, more aware of the people around him, and more in tune with his own capacity to spread joy.

Or consider the story of a woman named Evelyn, who decided to anonymously leave a bouquet of flowers on the doorstep of a neighbor she knew was going through a divorce. She didn't sign a card or tell a soul. A few days later, she overheard her neighbor saying how much the flowers had meant to her, giving her hope on a day when she felt utterly alone. Evelyn's silent kindness didn't need an audience to be powerful; it was the act itself that created a bridge of empathy and compassion.

How to Start Practicing Silent Kindness

You might be wondering how you can begin practicing silent kindness in your own life. Here are a few simple ideas to get started:

1. **Leave Kind Notes**: Write anonymous notes of encouragement or inspiration and leave them in places where people will find them—taped to a mirror in a public restroom, slipped into a library book, or left on a coworker's desk.

2. **Donate Anonymously**: If there's a cause or charity close to your heart, consider making an anonymous donation. It could be money, time, or resources—whatever you feel called to give.

3. **Help in Secret**: If you know someone who is struggling—perhaps a friend going through a tough time or a neighbor facing hardship—find ways to help without revealing your identity. Pay for a meal delivery, shovel their driveway, or send them groceries.

4. **Be a Silent Cheerleader**: Be the one who supports others from behind the scenes. Write positive reviews for small businesses, share job postings that might help someone in need, or recommend friends for opportunities, all without seeking acknowledgment.

Challenge: Embrace the Joy of Silent Kindness

This week, I challenge you to embrace the power of silent kindness. Choose one act of kindness that you can do anonymously and carry it out without anyone knowing. It could be as simple as leaving a compliment on a sticky note for a stranger or donating to a cause in secret. The goal is to do something that brings joy or relief to someone else without the need for recognition.

Notice how this feels. Pay attention to the joy that bubbles up inside you, the sense of quiet connection with the world around you. Reflect on how this act of silent kindness changes your perspective and deepens your understanding of what it means to truly give. Remember, kindness is not about being seen; it's about seeing others and letting them know they matter.

As you move forward, let silent kindness be your secret superpower—a way to make the world a little brighter, one quiet act at a time.

Silent kindness teaches us that the most profound connections happen when no one is watching, and the most meaningful changes occur in the spaces between words and actions. Give it a try. You might find that those invisible threads of kindness are the strongest of all.

CHAPTER 19
Lifting Others by Recognizing Their Achievements

Have you ever felt the thrill of someone genuinely celebrating your success? Maybe it was a friend cheering for you after a promotion, a coworker complimenting your hard work, or a loved one throwing you a small surprise for achieving a personal goal. Those moments matter. They make us feel seen, valued, and appreciated. Celebrating others is a simple but powerful act of kindness that lifts people up, strengthens our connections, and spreads positivity.

But in a world where we're often encouraged to focus on our own achievements, it's easy to underestimate the value of celebrating the successes of others. Yet, recognizing someone else's accomplishments doesn't diminish our own. In fact, it does quite the opposite: it builds a sense of community, fosters goodwill, and often inspires others to be their best selves. So, let's dive into why celebrating others is so transformative and how you can make it a part of your everyday life.

The Domino Effect of Recognition

Celebrating others is more than just a polite gesture —it's an intentional act of kindness that can have a far-reaching impact. When we take the time to acknowledge someone else's success, we're saying, "I see you. I value what you've done. You matter." This validation can be incredibly powerful.

Consider the story of Tom, a young manager at a small marketing firm. He made it a point to celebrate his team's achievements, big or small. When someone landed a new client, he didn't just send an email; he called them out in team meetings, expressing his genuine admiration for their efforts. On birthdays or work anniversaries, Tom would leave handwritten notes on his team members' desks, highlighting what he appreciated most about them. One day, a junior employee approached him, teary-eyed, saying, "No one has ever made me feel this valued at a job before." That moment reaffirmed to Tom that celebrating others wasn't just good for team morale—it was life-changing.

Why Celebrating Others Matters

There are several reasons why celebrating the achievements of others is so impactful:

1. **Boosts Self-Esteem and Confidence**: When someone's efforts are acknowledged, it boosts their

self-esteem and reinforces their confidence. It's like a pat on the back that says, "Keep going. You're doing great." This can be especially meaningful in challenging times when someone might be doubting themselves.

2. **Fosters Positive Relationships**: Recognition builds trust and strengthens relationships. When you genuinely celebrate someone else, you show that you care about their well-being and success. This fosters a sense of camaraderie and can deepen bonds between friends, colleagues, and family members.

3. **Inspires a Culture of Kindness**: Celebrating others creates a ripple effect, encouraging those around you to do the same. When you make a habit of recognizing others' achievements, it inspires those people to celebrate others too, spreading kindness like a domino effect.

4. **Promotes a Growth Mindset**: Recognizing others' achievements shifts our focus from a fixed mindset of scarcity to one of growth and abundance. It helps us see that there is enough success for everyone, reducing envy or competition and replacing it with a genuine sense of shared joy.

Practical Ways to Celebrate Others

Celebrating others doesn't have to be complicated or expensive. Here are some simple, practical ways to incorporate this habit into your daily life:

1. **Acknowledge Publicly and Privately**: When

someone achieves something, acknowledge it both publicly and privately. Send a congratulatory email or text, but also give them a shout-out in a group setting or meeting. This acknowledges that you truly appreciate their efforts.

2. **Give Personalized Compliments**: Instead of a generic "Good job," be specific about what you're recognizing. Say something like, "I'm really impressed by the creative solution you came up with for that problem" or "Your dedication and hard work really paid off on that project." This level of detail makes the compliment more meaningful and memorable.

3. **Celebrate Small Wins**: Not every celebration has to be for a major milestone. Recognize small victories, too—a colleague's successful presentation, a friend's new fitness routine, or a family member's progress on a personal goal. Small celebrations keep the momentum going and reinforce a positive atmosphere.

4. **Use Social Media Mindfully**: Share someone else's achievement on social media, but be thoughtful about it. Make sure it's something they'd be comfortable with and frame it in a way that truly honors their accomplishment, rather than just grabbing attention.

5. **Host a "Celebration Day"**: Choose a day each month to celebrate the achievements of people

in your circle. It could be a virtual gathering, a potluck, or even just a group chat where everyone shares what they're proud of or who they want to recognize. The goal is to create a space for positive acknowledgment.

6. **Write a Handwritten Note**: In an age of digital communication, a handwritten note stands out. Take a moment to write a thoughtful card to someone who has achieved something meaningful. Let them know you noticed their efforts and are proud of them.

Challenge: Make Celebrating Others a Habit

This week, I challenge you to make celebrating others a regular practice. Start with one person in your life —perhaps a friend, a coworker, or a family member. Think about something they've achieved recently and find a way to recognize it. It could be a thoughtful message, a small celebration, or simply a heartfelt compliment.

Notice how this act makes both you and the other person feel. Reflect on the impact of your recognition and how it strengthens your relationship. As you make this a habit, you'll find that celebrating others is a gift that keeps on giving—a simple yet profound way to spread kindness, joy, and encouragement in the world.

Celebrating others is a small act of kindness with a big impact. It's about choosing to lift people up, recognizing their efforts, and showing them they matter. So, let's make a habit of celebrating each other, spreading positivity, and building a world where everyone feels seen and valued. After all, in lifting others, we rise too.

CHAPTER 20
Kindness in Conflict: How to Be Gentle in Disagreements

Conflict is something most of us try to avoid. It can be uncomfortable, unsettling, and sometimes downright scary. Whether it's a disagreement with a coworker, a misunderstanding with a friend, or a heated argument with a loved one, conflicts have a way of bringing out our worst instincts. We feel our hearts race, our voices rise, and our defenses go up. But what if, instead of seeing conflict as a battle to be won, we approached it as an opportunity to practice kindness?

At first glance, kindness in conflict might seem counterintuitive. How can we be kind when emotions are high and tensions are thick? The truth is, approaching conflict with kindness doesn't mean avoiding difficult conversations or pretending everything is fine. It means engaging in these moments with a gentle heart and a genuine desire to understand. Let's explore how we can use kindness as a powerful tool to navigate disagreements and build stronger connections.

Why Kindness is Difficult in Conflict

Before we delve into strategies for being kind during disagreements, it's important to understand why it's so challenging in the first place. Our brains are wired for self-preservation. When we perceive a threat—be it a physical danger or an opposing opinion—our "fight or flight" response kicks in. This response might protect us in a life-threatening situation, but it's not so helpful during a disagreement.

When our adrenaline is pumping, it's easy to react with defensiveness, anger, or frustration. We feel compelled to "win" the argument, often at the expense of the relationship. Kindness, on the other hand, requires us to step out of this reactive mode and consciously choose a different path—one that fosters understanding, empathy, and connection.

1. Start with Curiosity, Not Judgment

One of the most effective ways to bring kindness into a disagreement is to start with curiosity instead of judgment. When someone expresses a viewpoint that clashes with your own, it's easy to jump to conclusions or make assumptions about their motives. Instead, take a deep breath and ask yourself, "Why might they feel this way?" or "What experiences have led them to this perspective?"

For example, if a friend makes a comment that stings, resist the urge to snap back with a defensive remark. Instead, try saying, "I hear what you're saying, but I'm curious about why you feel that way." This simple shift can open the door to a more productive conversation and show the other person that you're genuinely interested in understanding their point of view.

2. Use "I" Statements to Communicate Your Feelings

When we're upset, we often use "you" statements like, "You never listen!" or "You're always late!" These statements can feel accusatory and make the other person defensive, escalating the conflict.

Instead, try framing your feelings with "I" statements. For example, rather than saying, "You're never on time," you could say, "I feel frustrated when we're late because it makes me anxious." This slight shift in language can make a big difference. It allows you to express your feelings without blaming the other person, creating an environment where both of you can communicate openly and honestly.

3. Practice Active Listening

Active listening is one of the best powerful tools for diffusing conflict. Too often, we think we're listening when, in reality, we're just waiting for our turn to speak. Active listening means fully focusing on what the other person is saying, without interrupting, judging, or planning your response.

Try this: when someone is speaking, maintain eye contact, nod occasionally to show you're engaged, and resist the urge to interrupt. After they finish, summarize what you've heard by saying, "So, if I understand correctly, you're feeling upset because..." This not only shows that you're listening, but it also helps clear up any misunderstandings before they escalate.

4. Pause and Breathe

In the heat of the moment, it can be tempting to fire back a quick response. But a brief pause can work wonders. Take a deep breath, count to ten, or even excuse yourself for a few minutes if you need to. This short break gives you a chance to calm down and collect your thoughts.

You might say, "I really want to resolve this, but I need a moment to gather my thoughts." This approach demonstrates your commitment to a constructive conversation while also respecting your own emotional boundaries.

5. Find Common Ground

When in conflict, it's easy to zero in on what divides us. Instead, try looking for common ground. What are the shared goals or values that can help bring you together? Maybe you and a coworker disagree on a project's approach, but you both want the team to succeed. Or perhaps you and a friend have different political views, but you both value honesty and integrity.

Highlighting these shared elements can turn the conversation from "me vs. you" to "us vs. the problem." You might say, "I know we see this differently, but we both care about finding the best solution. Let's focus on that."

6. Apologize When Necessary

Nobody likes admitting they're wrong, but it's crucial for resolving conflicts and maintaining healthy relationships. If you realize that you've hurt someone, be quick to apologize. A sincere apology shows humility and a willingness to make amends.

Avoid using phrases like, "I'm sorry you feel that way," which can come across as dismissive. Instead, take ownership of your actions: "I'm sorry for what I said earlier. I realize it was hurtful, and I didn't mean to upset you." A heartfelt apology has the power to mend relationships and restore trust.

7. Keep the Bigger Picture in Mind

When we're deep in a disagreement, it's easy to lose sight of what truly matters. Ask yourself: Is winning this argument worth damaging the relationship? What are you really fighting for? Often, conflicts are less about the issue at hand and more about underlying emotions like fear, frustration, or hurt.

Shift your focus from the conflict to the relationship itself. You might say, "I value our friendship, and I don't want this disagreement to come between us. Let's find a way to work through this together." This perspective helps you stay calm, compassionate, and kind, even when the conversation gets tough.

8. Lighten the Mood with Humor

If the situation allows, a touch of humor can be an excellent way to defuse tension. A lighthearted comment or a shared laugh can remind both parties that the disagreement is not the end of the world. Just be careful that your humor is kind and inclusive, not at the expense of the other person.

For instance, if you and a partner are arguing over something minor, you might joke, "Well, at least we're both passionate, right?" A little humor can break the ice and help bring you back to a place of connection.

Your Call to Action

The next time you find yourself in a conflict, challenge yourself to approach it with kindness. Remember that kindness doesn't mean avoiding tough conversations or letting people walk all over you. It means engaging in those conversations in a way that is respectful, compassionate, and constructive.

Use curiosity instead of judgment, speak from your own experience, and practice active listening. Most importantly, keep the bigger picture in mind. By being kind in conflict, you can transform a challenging moment into an opportunity for growth, understanding, and deeper connection.

CHAPTER 21
Meeting Unkindness with Strength and Calm

Showing kindness can be difficult at times, especially when you're faced with unkindness. It's natural to want to react defensively or even lash out in response to rude remarks, angry gestures, or outright hostility. But what if there were another way? What if, instead of mirroring negativity, we chose to respond with kindness?

Choosing kindness in the face of unkindness is not about ignoring the wrong or pretending that everything is fine. It's about breaking the cycle of negativity and refusing to be dragged down by it. When we respond to unkindness with compassion, we not only change the dynamic of the interaction, but we also strengthen our ability to remain calm and grounded. This chapter explores the transformative power of choosing kindness in difficult situations and offers practical advice for how to make it happen.

The Power of Kindness Over Negativity

Imagine this: You're in a rush, trying to get through the grocery store checkout line quickly. You accidentally bump into someone's cart. The person turns around and snaps, "Watch where you're going!" In that moment, you have a choice. You could snap back, "Calm down! It was just an accident!" Or, you could take a breath, smile, and say, "I'm so sorry. I didn't mean to bump your cart. I hope you have a great day."

By choosing the second option, you create a different outcome. Instead of escalating the tension, you introduce calmness and empathy into the interaction. This response has the potential to disarm the other person's anger. They might still be upset, but your kindness could make them reconsider their own reaction. Perhaps they're having a bad day, or maybe they've been stressed out by something unrelated. By choosing kindness, you're giving them a chance to reset, to pause, and to possibly soften their stance.

The Strength of Staying Calm

It takes real strength to be kind in the face of unkindness. It's easy to react impulsively when you feel attacked or misunderstood. However, responding with kindness requires self-control, patience, and a willingness to see beyond someone's harsh words or actions.

Think of it like a muscle you have to train. The more

you practice remaining calm and compassionate when faced with unkindness, the stronger that muscle becomes. It's not about being passive or letting people walk all over you; it's about choosing your response intentionally. You're taking control of the situation, not letting someone else's negativity dictate your behavior.

A great example of this can be seen in customer service scenarios. Imagine a barista at a coffee shop who is greeted by an irate customer complaining that their coffee order was wrong. The customer is loud, rude, and clearly upset. The barista has two choices: react defensively or respond with kindness.

If the barista chooses the path of kindness, they might say something like, "I'm so sorry that your order wasn't right. Let me fix it for you right away, and I'd like to offer you a free pastry for the trouble." This simple act of empathy and understanding often diffuses the situation. The customer feels heard and validated, and their anger starts to melt away. In many cases, the customer ends up apologizing for their initial rudeness, or at least leaving with a more positive impression than when they came in.

Disarming Unkindness

Kindness has a way of catching people off guard. When someone expects hostility and instead encounters warmth, it can be a jarring but powerful experience. It disrupts their negative mindset and can make them think twice about their own behavior.

For example, consider a situation at work. You're in a meeting, and a colleague makes a dismissive remark about your idea. You feel the sting of embarrassment and anger rising, but instead of firing back, you calmly say, "I hear your concerns, and I'd love to understand your perspective better. Could you explain what you think could be improved?"

This unexpected response opens up a dialogue rather than closing it down with defensiveness. Your colleague might be taken aback but will likely appreciate your willingness to engage respectfully. More importantly, this approach can turn a potentially hostile exchange into a constructive conversation. You've disarmed the situation with kindness, turning a negative moment into an opportunity for growth.

Practical Ways to Choose Kindness

1. **Pause Before Reacting**: When faced with unkindness, take a deep breath and count to three. This brief pause gives you time to think about how you want to respond, rather than reacting impulsively.

2. **Put Yourself in Their Shoes**: Try to consider what might be motivating the other person's behavior. Are they stressed, tired, or dealing with a personal issue? Understanding their perspective can make it easier to respond with compassion.

3. **Use Gentle Language**: Instead of saying "You're

wrong!" try "I see it differently, and here's why." This approach reduces defensiveness and invites a more open discussion.

4. **Practice Empathy**: Show empathy by acknowledging the other person's feelings, even if you don't agree with their behavior. Saying something like "I can see you're upset, and I'm here to help if I can" demonstrates understanding without condoning rudeness.

5. **Walk Away When Necessary**: Sometimes, the best response is no response. If the situation is too heated, take a step back. You can choose to revisit the conversation later, when emotions have cooled.

Kindness in Motion: How One Act Can Change Many People

Kindness in the face of unkindness not only has the power to change individual interactions but can also create a domino effect that reaches far beyond the moment. When you choose kindness, you set an example for others. Your calm and compassionate response can inspire others to think about how they react in similar situations.

Imagine a world where, instead of reacting with anger or frustration, people chose to respond with understanding and empathy. The ripple effect would be profound—more peaceful interactions, less stress, and a greater sense of community and connection.

Call to Action: Practice the Pause

The next time you find yourself faced with unkindness, I encourage you to practice the pause. Take a moment to breathe, reflect, and choose how you want to respond. Remember that kindness is a choice—a powerful choice that can change the dynamic of any situation.

Try it for a week. Keep a journal of the moments when you consciously chose kindness over retaliation. Reflect on how it felt, both for you and the other person. Notice any changes in your mood, your stress levels, or the way others respond to you.

By practicing this kind of intentional kindness, you not only break the cycle of negativity but also strengthen your own resilience and compassion. You may not always change the other person, but you will always have the power to change yourself—and that's where true transformation begins.

CHAPTER 22

The Onion Principle: The Many Layers of Humanity

We've all encountered someone who, at first glance, left us with a less-than-pleasant impression. Maybe they seemed grumpy, aloof, or uninterested in engaging. It's all too easy to form quick judgments about such individuals, assuming they are inherently rude or unfriendly. However, more often than not, these initial impressions are merely the tip of the iceberg. People often wear protective layers to shield themselves from past hurts, insecurities, or the trials of life. To understand this better, consider the onion: its outer layers are often dry and papery, concealing a tender and flavorful core.

Think about the times you've felt misunderstood or unfairly judged by others based on a fleeting moment or a single interaction. We all experience days when we're short-tempered, distracted, or emotionally distant. In such moments, our behavior doesn't define our true character. Just as we hope others will grant us grace and understanding during our off days, we should extend the same courtesy to those around us. By looking beyond the surface, we can uncover the true essence of people.

Why We Protect Ourselves with Layers

People develop layers over time for various reasons —disappointments, fears, past traumas, or even the natural hardening that accompanies life's struggles. These layers act as a shield, much like the outer skin of an onion protects its delicate interior. They serve to guard individuals from emotional vulnerability and potential hurt. For instance, someone who has been hurt repeatedly may build a tough exterior to avoid further pain. They might appear distant or unapproachable, but this facade often masks a deeper, more sensitive self.

Yet, these defensive layers can also create barriers to genuine connection. When people put up walls, it becomes challenging for others to see their authentic selves, including the goodness and potential for meaningful relationships they possess. The problem is that these layers can prevent real interaction, leading to missed opportunities for deeper connections. By approaching others with patience, understanding, and compassion, we can begin to peel back these layers, revealing the beauty and depth that lies beneath.

How to Peel Back the Layers: Practical Advice

Uncovering someone's inner goodness requires effort and compassion. Here are some strategies to help you peel back the layers and connect more deeply with those around you:

1. **Lead with Curiosity, Not Judgment**
    When you encounter someone who seems cold or unapproachable, remind yourself that there's likely more to their story. Instead of jumping to conclusions, ask yourself, "What might this person be dealing with that I don't know?" Approach them with an open mind and heart, seeking to understand rather than to judge. Curiosity can lead to empathy, which in turn fosters connection.

2. **Practice Patience**
    Peeling back someone's layers is not an instantaneous process. It takes time to build trust and to move beyond their initial defenses. By being consistent and patient in your interactions, you create a safe environment that encourages others to gradually open up. Patience allows you to witness their true self over time, rather than making snap judgments based on a single encounter.

3. **Offer Genuine Kindness**
    Kindness is a powerful tool for breaking down barriers. Small acts of kindness, such as a smile, a thoughtful compliment, or a helping hand, can significantly impact someone's willingness

to let their guard down. Genuine kindness communicates that you care, which encourages others to reveal their true selves. It also helps to create a positive feedback loop, where kindness begets more kindness.

4. **Listen More Than You Speak**
    To understand someone's layers, it's essential to listen actively. Ask questions and listen without interrupting or jumping in with solutions immediately. This approach allows the person to express their thoughts and feelings fully, which can uncover the goodness beneath their exterior. Active listening demonstrates that you value their perspective and are invested in understanding their inner world.

5. **Give People Second Chances**
    First impressions are not always accurate. Just because someone has a rough day or appears off during an initial interaction doesn't mean they lack kindness or integrity. Giving people second (and even third) chances to show their true selves can lead to deeper, more meaningful connections. Recognizing that everyone has off days and extending the benefit of the doubt can open doors to more authentic relationships.

The Ripple Effect of Uncovering Inner Goodness

When we make the effort to look past the surface and uncover the inner goodness in others, it sets off a ripple effect. Your attempts to see people for who they truly are can inspire them to do the same for others. By approaching people with empathy and patience, you help foster a culture of understanding and acceptance, where individuals feel seen and valued for their true selves, not merely for their outward appearance.

This ripple effect extends beyond individual interactions. It can influence how we approach societal issues and engage with people from diverse backgrounds. When we see the humanity behind the defenses and struggles of others, we contribute to a more compassionate and connected community. By practicing the onion principle, we can collectively work towards a world where everyone is encouraged to reveal their authentic selves.

Call to Action

The next time you encounter someone who seems rough around the edges, remember the onion principle. While their exterior may not seem inviting, there's often something valuable hidden beneath the surface. People, like onions, may have layers of defenses, roughness, or sadness, but with a bit of patience, effort, and genuine kindness, you can uncover the goodness within.

By giving others the opportunity to reveal their true selves, you create possibilities for deeper and more meaningful connections. Ultimately, we all desire to be recognized for who we are inside—our hearts, our intentions, and our inherent goodness. By extending this perspective to others, you not only enhance their lives but enrich your own as well.

CHAPTER 23
The Gift of Time: Making a Lasting Impact

Time is one of the most valuable resources we have, and how we choose to spend it shapes our lives and the lives of those around us. In today's fast-paced world, it can feel like every minute is accounted for, leaving little room for anything else. But what if we looked at time differently? What if we saw our time not as something to guard closely, but as a gift we can give generously? Volunteering is one of the most powerful ways to share our time and create meaningful connections with others. When we volunteer, we step outside of ourselves and into a world of possibilities where we can make a real difference.

The Power of Volunteering

Volunteering is about more than just giving time; it's about offering a piece of yourself—your energy, your skills, and your presence—to a cause or a person who needs it. When you volunteer, you're saying, "I care about this, and I'm willing to invest in it." It's a profound act of kindness that has a ripple effect, spreading far beyond the immediate moment.

Volunteering can take many forms, from spending an afternoon at a local library or animal shelter to helping out at a community event or mentoring someone in need. No matter how you choose to volunteer, you're making a commitment to be present and contribute positively to your community.

Finding the Right Volunteer Opportunity

One of the great things about volunteering is that there are so many ways to do it. Whether you have a few hours a month or a few hours a week, there's A volunteer opportunity that matches your schedule and interests. Here are some ideas to help you find the right opportunity:

1. **Start Locally:** Look for volunteer opportunities in your local community. Check with nearby schools, libraries, hospitals, community centers, or non-profits. Many organizations are always looking for volunteers to help with events, programs, or day-to-day operations.

2. **Leverage Your Skills:** Consider how you can use your skills to make an impact. If you're a good writer, you might help a non-profit with grant writing or creating content. If you're a great cook, consider volunteering at a soup kitchen or baking

for a fundraiser. The skills you bring can make a big difference.

3. **Think About What You Love:** Volunteering should be enjoyable, not a chore. If you love animals, consider volunteering at a pet shelter. If you're passionate about the environment, look for local clean-up initiatives or conservation groups. Doing something you love will make volunteering feel rewarding, not burdensome.

4. **Be Open to New Experiences:** Volunteering is a great way to try something new. Maybe you've always been interested in gardening—why not volunteer at a community garden? Or perhaps you've wanted to improve your public speaking skills—consider reading to kids at a local library. Volunteering can be a path to personal growth as well as a way to help others.

The Chain Reaction of Volunteering: A Playful Spin

When you volunteer, you create a ripple effect that goes far beyond the immediate action. Think of it like tossing a pebble into a pond—the waves extend outward, touching more and more people. Your kindness can inspire others to act, creating a community of giving and compassion. Volunteering has the power to build bridges, foster understanding, and strengthen communities in ways that money never could.

Research shows that volunteering can improve your

mental and emotional well-being. It can reduce stress, increase happiness, and provide a deeper sense of purpose. When you give your time, you're not only helping others—you're also enriching your own life.

Volunteering as a Family or Group

Volunteering can also be a wonderful way to bond with your family and friends. Consider organizing a group volunteer activity. You could help prepare meals at a local homeless shelter, participate in a charity run, or work together on a community beautification project. These shared experiences create strong memories and reinforce a culture of kindness within your circle. Plus, it shows children the importance of giving back, teaching them valuable lessons about empathy, compassion, and community.

The Gift of Consistency

One of the most impactful ways to volunteer is by making a regular commitment. When you volunteer consistently, you build relationships, trust, and a deeper understanding of the cause you're supporting. Regular volunteers often become integral members of the teams they support, providing stability and reliability.

Consider committing to a specific day or time each week or month. This doesn't mean overcommitting yourself; even a couple of hours a month can have a significant impact. Consistency helps organizations plan better and provides the community with reliable support.

Combating Loneliness Through Volunteering

Loneliness is a growing problem in our society, and it affects people of all ages. Volunteering offers a solution, bringing people together in a meaningful way. When you volunteer, you're connecting with others, building relationships, and combating isolation—for yourself and for those you serve.

For example, volunteering at a senior center or visiting residents in a nursing home can provide companionship to those who might otherwise feel forgotten. Even a brief conversation or a shared cup of tea can brighten someone's day and give them a sense of belonging. Volunteering helps remind us that we are all part of something bigger and that our time and presence matter.

Volunteering Online

In today's digital age, volunteering doesn't always have to be in person. There are many opportunities to volunteer online, especially if you have limited mobility or prefer to stay at home. You could mentor a student over video calls, write letters to isolated seniors, or assist non-profits with digital marketing, social media, or website development. Virtual volunteering allows you to give your time from anywhere, expanding the ways you can make a difference.

Call to Action: Volunteer Your Time Today

Volunteering is a powerful way to practice kindness and make a positive impact. It's about sharing a piece of your life to help others, expecting nothing in return. The next time you find yourself with a free hour or two, consider how you might spend that time in service to others.

Reach out to a local organization, sign up for a community project, or simply offer your time to someone in need. Start small—an hour a week or a few hours a month can make a significant difference. The key is to start somewhere.

Remember, when you give your time, you're not only helping others—you're enriching your own life, building connections, and creating a kinder world. So, will you make the commitment to volunteer your time today? Your community needs you, and there's no better time to start than now.

CHAPTER 24
Building Bridges:
Embracing Diversity

In a world where we are more connected than ever, it's surprising how often we still feel divided. Whether it's because of race, religion, gender, age, or even lifestyle choices, differences can create invisible walls between us. But what if, instead of seeing those differences as barriers, we saw them as opportunities? Opportunities to build bridges that bring us closer to one another, to understand better, and to grow as individuals. That's where kindness comes in. Kindness is a powerful tool for embracing diversity, breaking down walls, and creating a world where everyone feels that they're being seen, heard, and valued.

The Challenge of Embracing Diversity

Let's face it: embracing diversity isn't always easy. It can be uncomfortable to step outside of our familiar circles and engage with people who have different beliefs, traditions, and perspectives. We tend to gravitate toward what we know, seeking comfort in the familiar. But that comfort zone can often limit our growth and the richness of our experiences.

It's human nature to feel a little uneasy when faced with something or someone new. Our brains are wired to be cautious of the unknown. But if we let those initial reactions stop us, we miss out on the incredible beauty and depth that diversity brings to our lives. And this is where kindness plays its role. Kindness encourages us to lean in, not pull away. It helps us move past the fear of the unknown and see the humanity in each other.

Kindness as a Bridge Builder

Think about a time when someone showed you kindness. Maybe it was a smile from a stranger, a genuine compliment, or someone listening to you without judgment. How did that make you feel? Kindness has a way of melting away defenses, of making us feel safe and accepted. Now imagine extending that same kindness to someone different from you. Imagine the walls that could come down, the connections that could be made, and the understanding that could grow.

When we practice kindness toward people who are different from us, we start to see the world through their eyes. We start to understand their struggles, joys, fears, and hopes. Kindness fosters empathy, and empathy is the foundation of genuine connection.

Practical Ways to Use Kindness to Embrace Diversity

So, how can we use kindness to bridge the gaps between us? Here are some practical steps:

1. Be Curious, Not Judgmental

Instead of making assumptions about someone based on their appearance, accent, or background, approach them with curiosity. Listen with an open mind and ask open-ended questions. For example, if you meet someone from a different culture, ask about their traditions or what they love most about their heritage. When we ask questions from a place of genuine curiosity, we show respect for their experiences and invite them to share their story. This simple act of kindness can open the door to meaningful conversations and new friendships.

2. Acknowledge and Challenge Your Biases

We all have biases; it's a natural part of being human. But the key is to recognize them and challenge them. Take a moment to reflect on any preconceived notions you might have about certain groups of people. Ask yourself where those beliefs came from and if they are truly fair or accurate. By being honest with ourselves and challenging our biases, we create space for kindness to grow. We start seeing people for who they are, not who we assume them to be.

3. Celebrate Differences

Instead of seeing differences as a source of division, celebrate them! Every culture, every person, has something unique to offer. Whether it's trying food from a different country, attending a cultural festival, or simply learning a new phrase in another language, find joy in the diversity around you. These small acts of appreciation show kindness and open your heart and mind to new experiences.

4. Stand Up Against Prejudice

Kindness isn't always passive. Sometimes, it requires courage to stand up against prejudice and discrimination. If you hear someone make a hurtful comment or see someone being treated unfairly because of their background, speak up. It doesn't have to be confrontational; it can be as simple as saying, "I don't think that's fair," or "We all deserve respect." Your words can make a significant impact and show kindness to those who need it most.

5. Be Inclusive in Your Actions

Inclusivity is kindness in action. When planning events, organizing meetings, or even just arranging a lunch outing, think about how you can make everyone feel welcome. Are you considering dietary restrictions, cultural preferences, or accessibility needs? Inclusivity shows that you care about others' well-being and comfort. It's a way of saying, "You belong here," and that simple message can mean the world to someone who feels different or left out.

Real Stories, Real Impact

Sometimes, a single act of kindness can make a lifetime of difference. Consider the story of Kevin, a man who grew up in a small town where he never met anyone from outside his community. When he moved to a big city for work, he felt overwhelmed and out of place. One day, he attended a community event and met Maria, who came from a completely different background. Instead of ignoring him, Maria approached him with a warm smile and asked him about his life, sharing stories of her own. That simple act of kindness made Kevin feel welcome, and it sparked a friendship that changed his perspective on diversity forever. Kevin learned to appreciate different cultures and now actively volunteers in community programs that celebrate diversity.

The Chain Reaction To Embracing Diversity With Kindness

When we choose kindness, we don't just impact the person we are kind to; we create a chain reaction. That one small act can inspire others to do the same. Imagine a world where every person, regardless of their background, feels valued and respected. Imagine the friendships formed, the creativity sparked, and the problems solved when diverse minds come together with kindness at the core. That is the power of kindness in embracing diversity.

A Call to Action: Your Kindness Challenge

Today, I am challenging you to step out of your comfort zone and practice kindness in a way that embraces diversity. Start a conversation with someone different from you, learn about their culture, or simply offer a smile to someone who looks like they might need it. Pay attention to your biases, celebrate the differences you see around you, and choose inclusivity in your actions.

Remember, kindness is a choice we make every day. It's a bridge that connects us, one human to another, across all the things that might otherwise divide us. So, let's build those bridges together, one kind act at a time.

By embracing diversity with kindness, we not only transform the world around us, but we also transform ourselves, becoming more open, compassionate, and understanding. And that, in itself, is a beautiful thing.

CHAPTER 25
Acts of Courage: Facing Rejection with Grace

Kindness is often seen as a simple, spontaneous act. Smile at a stranger, hold the door for someone, or compliment a coworker. But, if we're honest, many of us have felt a twinge of hesitation before reaching out with kindness. Why? Because we fear rejection. What if our smile isn't returned? What if our offer to help is met with a curt "no, thanks"?

The fear of rejection is deeply rooted in our human nature. It dates back to our ancestors, for whom rejection by the tribe could mean life or death. Today, however, the stakes aren't nearly as high, yet the fear still lingers. Understanding and overcoming this fear is crucial if we want to live a life filled with kindness.

Recognizing the Roots of the Fear

The first step to overcoming the fear of rejection when being kind is recognizing where it comes from. For many, it's tied to self-worth. When we extend a kind gesture and it isn't acknowledged or appreciated, it can feel like a personal affront. We take it as a sign that we're not good enough, that we've failed somehow. This fear is compounded by the fact that we live in a world that often emphasizes self-protection over vulnerability. We're taught to guard our hearts, avoid risks, and play it safe.

A New Perspective: Kindness as a Gift

Instead of seeing kindness as a transaction – something given in hopes of getting something in return – we can begin to see it as a gift. A gift given freely, without expectations. Imagine you give someone a present and they don't react as you hoped. Does that diminish the value of your gift? No. The value of kindness lies in the act itself, not in how it's received.

When we start to see kindness this way, it becomes easier to offer it without fear. Rejection becomes less of a threat because it's not about us. It's about the other person's readiness or capacity to receive. For example, if you offer to help a colleague and they decline, it could be that they want to complete the task themselves, not that they don't appreciate your kindness.

Real-Life Example: A Smile on the Subway

Take Lisa, a young woman who commuted to work on a crowded subway each day. She noticed a woman who seemed particularly weary, her shoulders slumped and her eyes downcast. Lisa felt an urge to offer a smile, but hesitated. What if the woman thought she was strange? What if she was met with a blank stare or worse, a frown?

One day, Lisa decided to overcome her fear and smiled at the woman anyway. To her surprise, the woman's face lit up, and she returned the smile with a heartfelt "Thank you." They didn't exchange words, but in that moment, something shifted. Lisa realized that her kindness had touched the woman in a small but meaningful way. Even if the woman hadn't responded positively, Lisa would have still felt good about reaching out. She had broken through her fear and offered kindness for its own sake.

Practical Strategies to Overcome the Fear

1. Start Small and Build Confidence

If the fear of rejection feels overwhelming, start with small acts of kindness that don't require much emotional risk. Pay a compliment to a barista, hold the elevator for a neighbor, or send a "thinking of you" text to a friend. Each time you perform a kind act, your confidence will grow, and the fear will diminish. You'll start to see that most people respond positively, and even when they don't, it's not a reflection on you.

2. Practice Self-Compassion

Being kind to yourself is crucial when facing the fear of rejection. Remind yourself that it's okay to feel afraid – everyone does at times. Instead of criticizing yourself for your fear, be gentle and understanding. Think about how you would comfort a friend who felt the same way. Self-compassion makes it easier to take risks and be kind, even when there's a chance of rejection.

3. Reframe Rejection as Redirection
Not every act of kindness will be warmly received, and that's okay. Instead of seeing rejection as a failure, reframe it as redirection. Maybe the person who declined your kindness simply wasn't in a place to receive it. That doesn't mean your kindness was wasted. In fact, it might be a sign that your kindness is needed elsewhere. Think of it as the universe guiding you to where you're most needed.

4. Remember, It's Not About You
One of the most liberating realizations is that other people's reactions to your kindness often have little to do with you. Everyone is dealing with their own struggles, stresses, and moods. A stranger's frown or an unreturned smile may have more to do with their bad day than with your gesture. Keeping this in mind helps you to not take things personally and to continue being kind, regardless of how others react.

5. Seek Out Stories of Kindness
Reading or hearing about the experiences of others who have faced their fears and acted with kindness can be incredibly motivating. For example, consider the story of David, who started writing anonymous

thank-you notes to people in his community – the grocery store clerk, the mail carrier, even the person who cleaned the public restrooms. At first, he was afraid his notes would be seen as weird or intrusive, but he decided to do it anyway. To his surprise, many people were touched by his gesture, and he began to receive thank-you notes in return. David's story reminds us that acts of kindness, even small ones, can have a ripple effect far beyond what we imagine.

Being Courageously Kind

Overcoming the fear of rejection when being kind is not about becoming fearless. It's about being courageous enough to act in the face of fear. It's about recognizing that kindness is a gift that has value in and of itself, regardless of how it's received. As we continue to practice kindness, we discover that the real reward lies not in others' reactions but in the joy and fulfillment we feel from living in alignment with our values.

So, the next time you feel that twinge of fear before extending a kind gesture, remember that you're not alone. Many others have felt the same but chose to be kind anyway. And in doing so, they found a deeper connection not just with others, but with themselves.

A Personal Challenge: Practice Kindness Despite Fear

If you're ready to take action, here's a challenge:

For the next week, commit to performing one act of kindness that feels slightly outside your comfort zone. It could be something as simple as giving a genuine compliment to a stranger or calling a family member you've been distant from. Pay attention to how you feel before, during, and after the act. Notice how the fear of rejection lessens over time and how the joy of giving grows.

CHAPTER 26

Respectful Defeat: The True Measure of a Competitor

We've all seen it happen—an athlete misses a crucial shot, a team loses in the final seconds, or a competitor stumbles just before the finish line. The disappointment is palpable. In sports, as in life, there are moments when things don't go our way. But what truly stands out is not just how we win, but how we handle defeat. Losing gracefully is an art, one that requires a great deal of kindness—toward ourselves, our opponents, and everyone around us.

Losing gracefully doesn't mean pretending you're not disappointed or frustrated. It means showing respect, empathy, and humility in the face of loss. It's about finding strength in adversity and recognizing that every game, every competition, is an opportunity to grow as a person. In this chapter, we will explore why kindness is a crucial part of sportsmanship, how to embrace losing with grace, and how it can positively impact not just the playing field but every aspect of our lives.

Why Kindness Matters in Sports

When we think of sports, we often think of competition, rivalry, and the desire to win. But sports also teach us some of the most important lessons about life: how to work as a team, how to push through challenges, and how to handle both victory and defeat. In many ways, sports are a microcosm of life itself, filled with moments of triumph and setbacks.

Kindness in sports is about more than just being a good sport. It's about showing respect for others, recognizing their efforts, and celebrating their successes even when they are not our own. Kindness fosters a sense of camaraderie, trust and mutual respect, fostering an environment where everyone feels appreciated, valued, regardless of the outcome.

Take the story of tennis legend Roger Federer, for example. Known for his grace both on and off the court, Federer often went out of his way to praise his opponents, even in defeat. After losing a particularly tough match to his long-time rival Rafael Nadal, Federer didn't sulk or make excuses. Instead, he congratulated Nadal with genuine warmth, acknowledging the hard work and skill that led to Nadal's victory. His behavior set a powerful example for fans and fellow athletes alike, showing that kindness and respect are not signs of weakness, but of true strength.

The Benefits of Losing Gracefully

Losing gracefully can be challenging, especially when we feel we've given everything we had, only to fall short. But embracing this practice has several benefits that go beyond the immediate moment:

1. **Builds Resilience**: When you lose gracefully, you learn to bounce back more quickly. Instead of dwelling on what went wrong, you concentrate on what you can learn and how you can grow. This mindset helps build mental toughness and resilience.

2. **Fosters Positive Relationships**: No one likes a sore loser. By accepting defeat with dignity, you show respect for your opponents and teammates, which strengthens relationships and builds a more positive community.

3. **Enhances Personal Growth**: Every loss is an opportunity to reflect on your performance and grow. It teaches humility and helps you understand that losing is not a reflection of your worth, but a step toward becoming better.

4. **Improves Emotional Intelligence**: Learning to manage your emotions in the face of loss improves your emotional intelligence, making you more empathetic and understanding toward others.

Real-Life Examples of Grace in Defeat

Let's look at another example from the world of sports. In 2016, during the Olympic women's 5000-meter race, runners Abbey D'Agostino from the United States and Nikki Hamblin from New Zealand collided and fell to the ground. Instead of focusing solely on getting back into the race, D'Agostino helped Hamblin to her feet, urging her to finish. Despite being in pain herself, D'Agostino's act of kindness became one of the most memorable moments of the Olympics, highlighting the importance of compassion over competition.

Their sportsmanship was recognized worldwide, showing that even in the heat of competition, kindness can shine through. It was a powerful reminder that the way we handle ourselves in moments of struggle often leaves a more lasting impression than any medal or trophy ever could.

Another example comes from the world of soccer. After losing a crucial match in the World Cup, Japanese fans stayed behind to clean up the stadium, while their team left a spotless locker room with a handwritten thank-you note to their hosts. Their actions sent a powerful message to the world: kindness and respect don't end when the final whistle blows.

How to Practice Losing Gracefully

So, how can we learn to lose gracefully, whether in sports or in life? Here are some practical tips to help you embrace kindness in moments of defeat:

1. **Acknowledge Your Feelings**: It's natural to feel disappointed or frustrated when things don't go your way. Allow yourself to feel these emotions without judgment. Recognize that it's okay to feel upset, but don't let it cloud your ability to be kind and respectful.

2. **Give Credit Where It's Due**: Whether you lose by a small margin or a large one, take a moment to acknowledge the efforts of your opponent. Congratulate them on their performance, and recognize their hard work and skill. This simple act can turn a moment of defeat into a moment of mutual respect.

3. **Reflect on the Experience**: After the game or competition, take some time to reflect on what you learned. What went well? What could you improve? Use this reflection as a tool for growth, rather than dwelling on the loss itself.

4. **Keep Perspective**: Remember that a single loss does not define you. It's just one moment in a much larger journey. Remind yourself that every athlete, every team, and every person experiences setbacks. It's how you respond to them that truly matters.

5. **Practice Self-Compassion**: Be kind to yourself in moments of defeat. Don't beat yourself up over mistakes or missed opportunities. Instead, show yourself the same compassion and understanding you would give to a friend.

6. Celebrate the Effort, Not Just the Outcome: Focus on the effort you put in, not just the end result. Recognize the hard work, dedication, and passion that brought you to that moment. Celebrate the journey, regardless of the outcome.

A Call to Action: Embrace the Kindness of Losing Gracefully

In sports, as in life, we all face moments of loss. But by choosing to lose gracefully, with kindness and respect, we become not just better athletes, but better human beings. Remember, it's not just about winning the game—it's about how you play it. And when you play it with kindness, you always win, no matter the score.

The next time you find yourself on the losing end, whether it's in sports, work, or any aspect of life, remember that how you handle that moment says more about your character than the loss itself. Choose kindness, show respect, and be gracious in defeat. Not only will you set a positive example for others, but you'll also find a sense of peace and growth within yourself.

Losing gracefully is not about minimizing your effort or accepting failure; it's about recognizing the value of every experience, every challenge, and every opponent as an opportunity for growth. It's about finding strength in humility and choosing kindness as your winning strategy.

CHAPTER 27

Being Kind Versus Being Right

Have you ever found yourself in a heated argument, fiercely defending your point of view, only to realize afterward that the conflict did more harm than good? Maybe you were "right," but you walked away feeling drained, upset, or disconnected from the person you were talking to. This is something we've all experienced at some point: the urge to prove we are right, even if it comes at the cost of our relationships.

In a world where everyone is trying to be heard, trying to be understood, and yes, trying to be right, we often forget that there is something far more powerful than being correct. Being kind.

The Need to Be Right

There is a certain satisfaction that comes with being right. It feels like a victory, like a validation of our thoughts and beliefs. In some situations, being right can indeed be important—think about life-and-death decisions or situations involving justice and fairness. But in many everyday situations, the need to be right can overshadow the bigger picture.

Take, for example, a story about a couple—Linda and Mark. They had been married for over 20 years, and like many couples, they sometimes argued about small things: which route to take to the store, how to load the dishwasher properly, or what the lyrics to a song actually were. One evening, they were hosting friends for dinner when they began to argue over a trivial fact about a movie they'd recently watched. What started as a minor disagreement escalated into an awkward and tense moment, overshadowing the entire evening. Linda later admitted that she had been so focused on proving herself right that she'd lost sight of what really mattered: enjoying a pleasant evening with friends and her husband.

Choosing Kindness Over Being Right

So why is it so hard to let go of the need to be right? It's because, in our minds, being right often feels like being respected or valued. But what if we could shift our focus? What if we could prioritize kindness and connection over being correct? Choosing kindness over being right doesn't mean you have to ignore your beliefs or opinions. It simply means you choose not to weaponize them.

Take another example, this time from a workplace setting. David, a manager at a small firm, was known for his sharp intellect and attention to detail. During a meeting, he noticed that one of his team members, Maria, had made a mistake in her report. He immediately pointed out her error in front of everyone, eager to correct her. While David was technically right, the way he handled the situation left Maria feeling embarrassed and unappreciated. Afterward, David realized he could have addressed the mistake privately and more gently. By prioritizing kindness, he would have maintained Maria's dignity and strengthened their working relationship.

Practical Steps to Practice Kindness

1. Pause and Reflect: The next time you feel the urge to prove you're right, take a moment to pause. Ask yourself: Is it worth it? Will this make the other person feel heard and respected? Sometimes, a brief pause is all it takes to choose kindness over confrontation.

2. Ask Questions, Don't Assume: Instead of jumping to conclusions or assuming you know everything, ask questions to understand the other person's point of view. Curiosity can turn potential conflicts into meaningful conversations.

3. Focus on the Bigger Picture: Consider what you are trying to achieve. Is the goal to connect, build trust, or maintain harmony? Focusing on the bigger picture often reveals that being right isn't the most important thing.

4. Use "I" Statements: When you do feel the need to share your perspective, try using "I" statements instead of "You" statements. For example, instead of saying, "You're wrong about this," try, "I see it differently because…" This small shift can make your communication feel less confrontational.

5. Embrace Empathy: Put yourself in the other person's shoes. Empathy allows you to see beyond the argument and recognize the feelings behind the words. Maybe the person you're disagreeing with has had a tough day or feels undervalued. When we lead with empathy, kindness naturally follows.

6. Practice Active Listening: Sometimes, people just need to feel heard. Even if you disagree, listening fully without planning your response can make the other person feel valued and respected.

Real-Life Examples of Choosing Kindness

One of the most touching examples of choosing kindness over being right comes from a story shared by a teacher named Rachel. She was teaching a class of first graders when a young boy named Timmy insisted that his birthday was on February 30th. Rachel knew there was no February 30th, but she also knew Timmy was a sensitive child who might feel embarrassed if corrected publicly. Instead of telling him he was wrong in front of the class, she smiled and said, "That's a very special day! Maybe we can celebrate your birthday together in class." Later, she gently explained the calendar to Timmy, in private, in a way that he could understand. By choosing kindness over correctness, Rachel maintained Timmy's confidence and trust.

Or consider the story of a customer service representative named Emily, who was dealing with a frustrated customer. The customer was upset about a policy that Emily couldn't change. She could have explained the rules and left it at that, but instead, she chose to listen with empathy. Emily acknowledged the customer's frustration and offered a small token —a discount code for the next purchase—as a gesture of goodwill. The customer left satisfied, even though Emily never admitted any fault on behalf of the company. Her kindness transformed the interaction from one of conflict to connection.

The Power Of Being Kind Versus Being Right

Kindness is powerful because it has the ability to change our interactions and relationships for the better. When you choose kindness, you encourage others to respond in kind. Imagine a world where more people placed a higher value on kindness than on being right. Conflicts would be less intense, relationships would grow stronger, and our everyday encounters would become more positive and meaningful.

This doesn't mean we should never disagree or avoid tough conversations. Rather, it means approaching these situations with an open heart and a spirit of understanding. We remind ourselves that the other person is also a human being, with their own experiences, challenges, and emotions.

Call To Action

So, the next time you find yourself in a debate, whether it's with a friend, family member, or stranger, take a deep breath and ask yourself: "Is being right more important than being kind?" The answer might surprise you. You may find that by letting go of the need to be right, you gain something far more valuable—a sense of peace, a stronger connection, and the satisfaction of knowing you chose to be kind.

Remember, kindness is a choice. And when we choose it, we not only change the world around us but also transform ourselves in the process.

CHAPTER 28
Generational Kindness: Passing It Down

Just imagine yourself standing at the edge of a dense forest, looking out at rows of tall, sturdy trees. These trees didn't just appear overnight. They grew over time, nourished by the sun, rain, and rich soil, with each new season adding another ring to their trunks. Like those trees, kindness is something that grows over time, passed down from one generation to the next. It's a legacy we can leave, and it's a gift we can give — a gift that keeps on giving.

When we think about the values we hope to pass on to our children or grandchildren, kindness often tops the list. We want them to be compassionate, thoughtful, and empathetic. But how do we ensure that kindness becomes a natural part of who they are? It starts with us, and it starts now.

The Ripple Effect of Kindness

We've all heard about the ripple effect — how a single act of kindness can spread far beyond its initial impact. Think about the last time someone held the door open for you or offered you a genuine compliment. Chances are, it lifted your spirits and made your day a little brighter. You might have even passed that good feeling along to someone else, whether by smiling at a stranger or being more patient with a coworker.

This ripple effect isn't just a phenomenon among adults; children observe and imitate our actions. When they see us being kind — helping a neighbor, speaking gently, or showing compassion — they learn to value kindness. They understand, through our example, that kindness isn't just a nice thing to do; it's the right thing to do.

Sharing Stories of Kindness

Stories are a powerful tool for teaching kindness. Think back to the tales you were told as a child — those that taught you about the importance of helping others, standing up for what's right, or simply being a good friend. Stories shape our understanding of the world and help us make sense of complex emotions and situations.

Make it a habit to share stories of kindness with the young people in your life. These don't have to be elaborate or dramatic; they can be simple, everyday acts. Share stories from your own life, or read books that celebrate kindness. Talk about how it feels to give and receive kindness and the impact it has on both parties. Through stories, children learn that kindness isn't just an abstract idea but rather an actual, tangible force that can change lives.

Making Kindness a Family Tradition

Traditions help us feel connected to our families and communities, and they provide a sense of continuity and belonging. Why not make kindness a family tradition? This could be as simple as having a "kindness jar" where each family member writes down an act of kindness they performed or witnessed and shares it during a weekly meal.

Another idea is to create a family kindness challenge. Set a goal to perform a certain number of kind acts each week or month. Celebrate these acts together, reinforcing the idea that kindness is something to strive for and be proud of.

Remember, traditions don't have to be grand or complicated. Even the smallest gestures can help build a culture of kindness in your family.

Teaching by Doing

Children learn best by doing, not just by hearing or seeing. Encourage them to take part in activities that require kindness, like volunteering at a local charity, helping a neighbor with yard work, or simply writing a note of appreciation to a teacher or friend.

Get creative and find ways to integrate kindness into daily life. For instance, you could create a "kindness scavenger hunt" where children have to find opportunities to be kind throughout their day. This could include picking up litter at the park, sharing toys with a sibling, or saying something nice to someone who seems sad. The key is to make kindness feel fun and rewarding.

Modeling Kindness in Everyday Moments

We don't have to wait for grand gestures to model kindness; it's often the small, everyday moments that matter most. Think about how you react when someone cuts you off in traffic, when you're frustrated with customer service, or when a friend cancels plans at the last minute. These are all opportunities to show the young people in your life what kindness looks like, even when it's not easy.

Children pick up on our behavior more than we realize. They see how we treat people who can do nothing for us, how we talk about others when they're not around, and how we respond to mistakes — both ours and others'. When we model kindness in these everyday moments, we teach them that kindness isn't just an option; it's a way of life.

Encouraging Empathy

Empathy is the foundation of kindness. It's the ability to put ourselves in someone else's shoes and understand their feelings. One of the best ways to nurture empathy in children is to encourage them to think about how their actions affect others.

Ask questions like, "How do you think that person felt when you helped them?" or "How would you feel if someone did that for you?" These questions help children develop a deeper understanding of emotions and build a habit of considering others' feelings before acting.

Creating Safe Spaces for Kindness

It's important to create an environment where children feel safe to express kindness. Sometimes, children may fear that being kind will make them appear weak or vulnerable. Encourage open conversations about these fears. Share your experiences and reassure them that kindness is a strength, not a weakness.

Praise acts of kindness, no matter how small, and let them know that kindness is valued in your family. When children see kindness being celebrated, they are more likely to embrace it themselves.

The Long-Term Benefits of Generational Kindness

Passing down kindness is not just about creating a more compassionate next generation; it also benefits us in the here and now. Studies have shown that people who practice kindness experience reduced stress, improved mental health, and even longer lifespans. When we commit to passing down kindness, we create a positive cycle that not only enhances our lives but also the lives of those around us.

We all have the power to shape the future by planting seeds of kindness today. Imagine a world where kindness is the norm, not the exception — a world where compassion, empathy, and generosity flow freely from one generation to the next.

Call to Action: Plant Your Seed of Kindness

Today, I invite you to think about the legacy of kindness you want to leave. What small acts can you start practicing today that will set an example for those who come after you? Share a story of kindness, create a family tradition, or simply be mindful of how you treat others in everyday situations.

Remember, the smallest seed can grow into the mightiest tree. By passing down kindness, we're planting seeds that will flourish for generations to come. Let's start today — one act, one moment, one day at a time.

CHAPTER 29
Embracing Imperfection on the Journey of Kindness

We often strive to live up to the highest ideals, especially when it comes to being kind. We read books like this, make resolutions to be better, and set goals to treat others with more compassion. But as with any journey, there are times when we stumble. We lose our patience, we speak a little too harshly, or we walk past someone who could have used our help. And in those moments, it's easy to feel like we've failed.

However, there's an important truth that we must remember: no one is perfect. The path to kindness, just like any worthwhile endeavor, is full of detours, stumbles, and setbacks. The real measure of our growth isn't in never making mistakes—it's in how we respond when we do.

The Perfection Myth

One of the most damaging beliefs is that we

should never falter when striving to be kind. We often hold ourselves to an impossibly high standard, expecting to handle every situation with grace and understanding. But the truth is, we're human. We get tired, we feel stress, and sometimes we simply make the wrong decision in the heat of the moment. Expecting perfection from ourselves sets us up for failure because it's unattainable. Even the kindest people falter, and that's okay.

It's not about being flawless in our kindness, but about how we recover when we fall short.

Recognizing and Acknowledging Your Missteps

When you recognize that you've missed an opportunity for kindness or acted in a way that didn't align with your values, the first step is simple: acknowledge it. There's no need to bury the moment or pretend it didn't happen. We all make mistakes, and acknowledging those mistakes is part of the growth process.

Take a deep breath and reflect on what happened. Was it a moment of stress? Were you distracted or overwhelmed? Did you react out of habit rather than intention? This reflection is crucial because it helps you understand why the misstep happened, which can inform how you move forward.

Importantly, this acknowledgment should come without judgment. It's not about beating yourself up or feeling guilty for not being perfect. It's about observing what happened, taking responsibility, and deciding to learn from it.

Reframing Failures as Opportunities

Every time we falter in our quest to be kind, we're given a new opportunity. It might not feel like it at the moment, but our mistakes are powerful teachers. They show us where we can improve and remind us that we're always learning. Instead of viewing these moments as failures, try reframing them as valuable lessons. Ask yourself, "What can I learn from this?" or "How can I handle this situation differently next time?"

For instance, if you snapped at a coworker in frustration, you now have the chance to recognize the triggers that led to that moment. Maybe it was stress, a lack of sleep, or frustration over something unrelated. By understanding these factors, you can better prepare for similar situations in the future and approach them with greater kindness and patience.

Mistakes are an inevitable part of growth. If you never made a mistake, you wouldn't have the opportunity to learn and become more mindful in your actions. The next time you falter, try to see it as a stepping stone on your journey rather than a roadblock.

Forgiving Yourself

Perhaps the hardest part of faltering in kindness is learning to forgive yourself. We often extend compassion to others but are far harsher on ourselves.

After all, you may think, "I should know better by now." But this internal criticism isn't helpful. In fact, it often makes it harder to get back on track.

True growth requires self-compassion. Just as you would forgive a friend for an off moment, you must learn to forgive yourself. It's okay to be imperfect. It's okay to make mistakes. What matters most is your intention to do better, not your ability to be flawless.

When you falter, remind yourself that you're still on the path. Being kind to yourself is just as important as being kind to others. Offer yourself the grace to move forward without the weight of guilt dragging you down.

The Call to Action: The Next Time You Falter

Now that you've recognized that faltering is a part of the journey, it's time to take action the next time you miss the mark. Here's a simple guide for how to respond when you find yourself falling short in your quest for kindness:

1. **Pause and Breathe** – When you realize you've faltered, stop for a moment. Take a few deep breaths to center yourself and create space to reflect.

2. **Acknowledge the Moment** – Without judgment, recognize what happened. "I was too impatient," or "I didn't offer help when I could have."

3. **Reflect on the Cause** – Ask yourself what led to the moment. Was it stress? Fatigue? Distraction?

Understanding the root cause helps you address it in the future.

4. **Reframe It as a Learning Opportunity** – Instead of focusing on the mistake, think about what you've learned. How can you approach a similar situation differently next time?

5. **Forgive Yourself** – Offer yourself the same kindness and compassion you would to a friend. Let go of the guilt and remind yourself that growth takes time.

6. **Get Back in Gear** – Don't dwell on the misstep. Decide to move forward with a renewed commitment to kindness. You've acknowledged the moment, learned from it, and now it's time to get back on track.

A Lifelong Journey

Remember, kindness isn't a destination. It's a lifelong practice, and like any practice, it comes with ups and downs. There will be days when you feel like you're embodying the spirit of kindness in every interaction. And there will be days when you fall short. That's okay. What matters most is your commitment to continue, to pick yourself up when you falter, and to keep moving forward.

As you navigate the path of kindness, give yourself permission to be imperfect. Celebrate your successes, learn from your missteps, and above all, extend the same kindness to yourself that you seek to offer the world.

CHAPTER 30

Bringing It All Together

Congratulations! You've reached the final chapter of this journey, and that's a significant achievement. Over the past 30 days, you have dived deep into what it truly means to live with kindness. You have explored how to listen with an open heart, uplift others with sincere words, reach out to strangers, show compassion online, and extend grace in the face of conflict. You've taken the time to challenge yourself, reflect on your actions, and hopefully experienced some transformative moments along the way.

But while this may be the last page of the book, it is certainly not the end of your journey. In many ways, it's just the beginning. The kindness you've explored and practiced is not a one-time project or a temporary experiment. It's a choice you make every day, a habit you cultivate over time, and a legacy you leave behind.

Choosing kindness means looking beyond yourself and extending grace, patience, and love—even when it's hard, inconvenient, or seemingly unnoticed.

The Real Work Begins Now

You've read the chapters, taken on the challenges, and felt inspired. But here's the truth: living kindly is not always easy. There will be moments when you falter. Maybe you'll find yourself snapping at a loved one after a long day, or failing to smile at a stranger in passing. You might miss an opportunity to help someone in need, or you might get so caught up in your own worries that kindness feels like the last thing on your mind.

These moments are normal, and it's important to remember that kindness is a lifelong process, not a one-time event. Like any other worthwhile endeavor, it comes with its share of setbacks. You won't always get it right, and that's okay. The goal is not to aim for perfection but to commit to growth. When you stumble, acknowledge it, learn from it, and then get back up and try again. Think of kindness like a muscle —the more you use it, the stronger it gets.

Consider each challenge you faced over the past month as a tool added to your toolkit. When you're feeling impatient or frustrated, you can draw upon the lesson from "Listening with Heart: The Gift of Being Present." When you're navigating a heated disagreement, you can apply the strategies from "Kindness in Conflict: How to Be Gentle in

Disagreements." If you find yourself scrolling through social media, remind yourself of "Navigating the Online World with Grace."

Each chapter has offered you different ways to practice kindness, but now it's up to you to weave these lessons into your daily life. Keep in mind that small acts of kindness can have a ripple effect far beyond what you can see. A simple smile, a sincere compliment, or a few minutes of your time can brighten someone's day in ways you may never fully realize. By continuing to practice these small acts, you create an environment where kindness is the norm, not the exception.

Kindness is a Choice, Every Day

Kindness is a choice you make, not just once, but over and over again. It's the decision to slow down and really listen when someone is speaking, even if you're in a hurry. It's choosing to give the benefit of the doubt when someone is unkind, recognizing that they too have their struggles. It's the conscious effort to lift up others rather than tear them down, especially when it would be easier to stay silent or walk away.

It's also about being kind to yourself. There will be days when you feel like you've failed in your efforts to be kind. Days when you snap at someone in a moment of frustration, or forget to thank the cashier at the grocery store. On these days, it's important to practice self-compassion. Remember that you are human, and being human means you are wonderfully imperfect.

Acknowledge your mistakes, learn from them, and forgive yourself so you can move forward.

Kindness as a Way of Life

To make kindness a way of life, it needs to become a natural part of your daily routine. This might mean setting aside a few minutes each morning to reflect on how you can show kindness throughout the day, or journaling each evening about the kind acts you witnessed or experienced. You might find it helpful to set small, specific goals for yourself, such as complimenting three people each day, or volunteering once a week. These small steps, when taken consistently, can help reinforce the habit of kindness.

It's also important to remember that kindness is not confined to grand gestures. Often, the simplest acts carry the most profound impact. Holding the door open for a stranger, offering a sincere compliment or simply being a good listener—these actions may seem small, but they can mean the world to someone else.

The Ripple Effect of Kindness

Your kindness can set off a ripple effect, extending far beyond what you can see. When you are kind to others, it inspires them to be kind in return, setting off a chain reaction that can positively affect countless lives. By choosing kindness, you are contributing to a world that is more compassionate, empathetic, and connected.

But the greatest reward of all is the transformation that happens within you. When you practice kindness regularly, you begin to see the world differently. You start to notice the beauty in ordinary moments, appreciate the uniqueness in every person you meet, and find joy in giving rather than receiving. Your heart becomes more open, your mind more empathetic, and your spirit more resilient.

Moving Forward with Kindness

As you move forward, let each day be an opportunity to infuse kindness into your life. Embrace this journey with an open heart, knowing that every act of kindness, no matter how small, can transform the world around you. Kindness is a lifelong commitment, not just a fleeting gesture. Let your light shine brighter with every choice and action. Continue with courage and hope, and you will uncover the essence of a **happier, calmer and more meaningful life**.